I0120254

Khoshru Navrosji Banaji

Memoirs of the late Framji Cowasji Banaji

Khoshru Navrosji Banaji

Memoirs of the late Framji Cowasji Banaji

ISBN/EAN: 9783337177591

Printed in Europe, USA, Canada, Australia, Japan

Cover: Foto ©ninafisch / pixelio.de

More available books at **www.hansebooks.com**

OF THE LATE

FRAMJI COWASJI BANAJI.

BY HIS GREAT GRANDSON

KHOSHRU NAVROSJI BANAJI.

𝔅𝔬𝔪𝔟𝔞𝔶:
PRINTED AT THE
BOMBAY GAZETTE STEAM PRINTING WORKS.

1892.

(All rights reserved.)

To

Dr. THOMAS BLANEY, J.P.,

&c. &c. &c.

Who has always evinced a great
interest in the welfare of the
Parsee Community, and to whom the
writer has been long connected
by ties of friendship,
this work has been humbly dedicated
as a token of the appreciation of his
many noble qualities,
by his friend and admirer,

K. N. BANAJI.

CONTENTS.

INTRODUCTION.

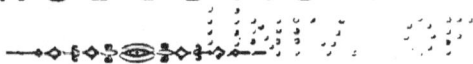

My aim in this book is to save from oblivion the memoirs of the late Framji Cowasji Banaji, whose long and splendid career has long since ended, and he has departed this transient life, for a happier one in the next. This will at once convey to the mind of many, that the capacity of a near relative, in which I stand to the deceased gentleman, has induced me to undertake this difficult task ; but I think, I cannot pay a better tribute of respect to his memory, than to draw out his memoir in an impartial light, holding up at the same time his good and amiable qualities, for the imitation, as well as the admiration, of the public. For a life of his, there has been a public call, for the sudden gloom, which overspread the Indian communities here, by his death, had called forth the sweetest expressions of sorrow, mingled with the admiration of his many good and noble qualities, not only from the Parsee community, of which he was for a very long time the cherished friend and champion, and on whom they looked with pride and endearment, as a patriarch, but from every other caste.

Indian biography is almost a novel thing among the natives here, and the difficulties, besetting the path of a person, undertaking to write out an Indian biography, are so many that the person, weary of his task, leaves the subject aside, and so, many brilliant personages in Indian History have been left to the working scythe of time, to work out its mouldering decay, and consequently many eminent personages have been altogether blotted out from memory, leaving, if any, very faint recollections, as mere hearsays of their past and brilliant deeds,

The Parsees do, indeed, boast of at present of having in bygone times, persons like a Dadysett, and Maneckji Sett, a Pestonji and a Hormasji Wadia, Sir Jamshedji Jeejibhoy Bart, and many others, who had, by their individual enterprise, raised themselves from obscurity to distinction ; but alas ! their distinctions have died with them, and no records are now left for us to judge of them, and such will still be the case with many more, until the taste of the Indian communities be refined.

The present case of Framji would have fallen a sacrifice to the same prevailing spirit, had I not kept firm and stable in my resolve. It is, therefore, my object to furnish to the public an impartial picture of one, whom they held in high veneration, and I fully trust that it will bear with it the solemn stamp of impartiality and truth. However humble may be my merits, the value of my contribution cannot be estimated too highly, if by only stating the facts with a careful accuracy, and drawing the inferences therefrom, it will be a lesson to those who have acquired an unrivalled ascendency over their countrymen, and with whom the welfare of their country is closely connected, to regard their duties as of paramount importance to their own personal interests, while on the other hand it will be a signal punishment to those who in such positions are entrapped in vices, and therefore have become the slaves of ambition and avarice.

The many objections in the way of undertaking this work have made the attempt a very difficult one, though it may not be found to be altogether hopeless. Thus labouring under a choice of evils, I have at last made up my mind to write out this life or memoir of one, whom I hold in high estimation, and to whom I am mostly endeared by ties very sacred—viz., of parentage ; but nothing of these will in any way act prejudicially upon my mind, in giving out a true narrative of facts, which distinguished this great and good man,—great and good we call him, because his many good and amiable qualities had truly rendered him great and good.

I could have gladly given over the task to a mere stranger, but in so doing, I would be transferring it to hands, who could not have been actuated by any feelings of a personal kind towards the deceased, and thus the subject would have been left to one, who, if not altogether incapable of performing it satisfactorily, at least, would do it incomparably inferior in the giving of that vivid likeness in its true and graphic colours.

At least this memoir, though not claiming to itself the high merits of history, may itself furnish sufficient materials for the purpose ; as the rise of this revered gentleman has been one of the most remarkable epochs in the history of the Parsee community, since they have come more and more in contact with the more civilized nations of the West, and were held to be the most enterprising people in India as to its future advancement, which I may safely and with pride say has been realized to a very great extent by that community alone. It may at the same time furnish future writers with facts illustrative of the times, unbiased with any influence to work out upon them, from other contemporary testimonies.

I may here conscientiously declare, that I have considered this a very sacred duty to perform, and have therefore attempted, as much as it lay in my power, to adhere to the truth, and give a true and faithful resemblance of the character, without either exaggeration or concealment, and have at the same time attempted to write this, as if, I were in no immediate connection with the deceased gentleman ;

but notwithstanding this, if any prejudices of a personal kind have acted upon my mind, I, in fact, am altogether unconscious of them.

I have great pleasure in acknowledging the obligation I owe to my much esteemed and respected father, the late Naorosji Nanabhoy Framji, who with tender and reverent care gathered together and recorded the particulars of this memoir.

In conclusion, I take this occasion of acknowledging my warm thanks for the kindness and courtsey, with which H. E. the Right Hon'ble Lord Northbrook, K.G., C.S.I., &c., has assisted me in my work, and also my cousin, Mr. Heerjibhoy Maneckji Rustomji of Calcutta, who has from the beginning evinced a great and lively interest in this work. I must further own the assistance I have received from the valued work, " *The Parsee Prakash*," of my friend Mr. Bomanji Byramji Patel.

K. N. B.

CHAPTER I.

The origin and establishment of the Banaji family in Bombay. Framji's ancestors. Their connection with the Dady Setts.

First of all, I will attempt to give a brief sketch of the birth and parentage of our memoir. Though I have been labouring, day after day, to collect all the possible facts related to this, yet I have failed, and failed materially, notwithstanding which I will try to do the best, with what little I already know about it.

The late Framji Cowasji Banaji, whose death has been a subject of regret with the European and Native communities, not only of Bombay, but of the Mofussil also, belonged to the Family of Banaji, which, with that of Wadia and Dadysett, have been long distinguished for their wealth and commercial enterprise ; and in works of charity and benevolence, have been second only to that very remarkable man, Sir Jamsetji Jeejibhoy, Bart.

Although Framji never had the wealth with which to provide for the physical comfort of his countrymen—he was very constantly foremost in energy, for their mental culture and moral improvement, as will be seen later on, when his life is narrated in connection with the Native Education in Bombay.

The present family surname derives its origin from one of the elderly and distinguished members of this family by the name of Banaji, who was the great grand-father of the deceased. As to the exact date of the establishment of this family in Bombay, nothing as to ensure certainty is at present known.

This family can at present trace its antiquity to upwards of a century, beyond which it is a known fact no other Parsee family of any consequence can at the present day boast to trace its antiquity.

Banaji Limji, the great grand-father of Mr. Framji, was the true founder of the Banaji Family. He came to Bombay about the year 1690 from the village of Bhagva_ dandee near Surat,and took some service under the East India Company. Shortly after, he left the desk for mercantile enterprise, and opened his own firm and carried on extensive business under the name and style of " Banaji Limji." He was the first Parsee gentleman who is said to have travelled over the sea to Pegu for extending his business. The first Parsee Panchayat was formed in his time, and he was elected their president. Mr. Banajee was consequently known by the familiar name of Davar. He died on the 30th July 1734, at the age of 80.

The ancient monument perpetuating the name of this family, now existing in Bombay, raised by its founder Banaji, is the small Fire-temple, called after the name of Banaji, " The Banaji Adarian " or Agiari, built about 25th June 1709. This Agiari having come to a delapidated condition, the members of the Banaji family subscribed a fund amongst themselves of Rs. 23,000 and thoroughly re- built it on the 15th of April 1845, Framji and his brothers Curshedji and Rustomji each having contributed Rs. 5,000.

Prior to the establishment of this family in Bombay under their ancestor Limji, they had resided in " Bhagwa " a small village, in the vicinity of Surat. This family has also received the surname of the " Goga," the origin of which is a very late one, and at the same time a very curious one. Cowasji Bawa (as he was familiarly called), the father of the deceased, was carrying on an extensive

trade with " Goga " the chief mart in Gujrat, from which
he received the surname of "Goga." While there are
some who attribute it to the hoarse voice of Cowasji. It so
happened, that on one occasion a dispute arose between Mr.
Cowasji and an Englishman, when Mr. Cowasji in a rage
said in a hoarse tone, " Go ! Go ! " and hence his friends
nicnamed him " Goga." Whatever be the origin of this
surname, the surname itself is a very curious one, and
neither Framji nor his brothers liked to be called by
that epithet : they, therefore, generally assumed for themselves the ancient family surname of " Banaji," which the
deceased also used in his signature.

Tracing the ancestries of this family, I come to Limji,
beyond which nothing is known, and even, what little is
known, is very uncertain and doubtful. No authanticated
particulars of Limji are to be found at the present day,
except those already stated below.

Banaji had three sons, of whom Byramji the eldest had
five sons, viz., Nanabhoy, Muncherji, Dadabhoy, Rustomji,
and Cowasji.

Byramji was one of the most distinguished members of
this family. He joined his father's business in the firm of
Banaji Limji in 1734. It is believed that in his time Dady
Nusservanji, afterwards deservedly called Dady Sett, came
to Bombay. He was employed by Byramji, who had great
regard for him, and it is believed that Dady first took a
start under Byramji, and after his death, began to carry
on an extensive trade on his own personal risk in China,
and other places ; as also being at the same time, held in
high estimation by the Company's agents here, who were
carrying on extensive trade in their monopoly acts at the
time, and was one of their principal Dubashes or brokers.
Like his father, Byramji was also the President of the

Parsee Panchayat. He died at the age of 72, on the 12th of May 1753. A Parsee writer in a letter to one of his European friends speaks of Dady Sett as follows :—

" Late Dady Sett, it may well and safely be said, was the founder of the Parsee eminence in Bombay. He was the first, who by his enterprise in commerce in connection with the European merchants of the day, the late Daniel Scott & Co., of England, and Adamson & Co., of Bombay, and by his other acts of munificence, for which he was pre-eminently distinguished 60 years ago, first drew the attention of the Europeans towards Parseemen's enterprise and rendered Bombay from that date " Parseemen's Glory."

It is believed that Dady's immediate ancestors were not in so good circumstances as himself, for it is known that his father followed the profession of a petty Dubash, and it was principally under Byramji Banaji that Dady began to prosper, and after his death, took up all the business which Byramji had carried on, and extended it by his own peculiar intellect and bold enterprise in commerce. Dady has been also remarkable for his singular generosity and benevolence of spirit. It is said that in his time the Parsee Fire-temple, which is known by the name of the " Dady Sett's Atash Behram," was first proposed to be built conjointly by Dady and some of the influential members of the Parsee community, chiefly of the Wadia family, who had all agreed to throw off that invidious distinction of sect—the Rushmees, and the Cadmees—and acknowledge the Cadmee date as the correct date, which would have been much to the advantage of both parties, and would have at the same time reconciled the ill-feelings ; but unfortunately on account of some disputes regarding the heavy expenses incurred on it, the other parties kept aloof, and Dady himself, much to his credit, though his circumstances were not very easy at the time, bore the costs of its erection, and completed this work of National Worship for his sect of the Parsees. This was the first "Atash Behram" of the Parsees in Bombay built on the 17th day of the first month of the year 1153 Yazadazard (of the Cudmee sect) *i.e.,* 29*th September* 1783.

It will thus be seen, that Dadysett owed his rise to the family of Banaji, but he did not forget the obligation, he was labouring under an obligation to this family, for in his own days of power, he repaid that obligation amply, by supporting the young members of this family, amongst whom was Framji. Framji readily acknowledged this, as will be seen from the following extract of a letter written by him to Thomas Wedding, Esq., dated 29th August 1821, on a separation of his partnership with Curshedji and Jehangir Ardeshir Sett :—

DEAR SIR,

Considering you to be one of my sincere old friends, who at all times will promote my views, and contribute to my welfare, under these circumstances I address you an account of some misunderstanding which took place between Curshedji and Jehangir Ardeshir and myself, of which I shall state here the particulars.

Since the death of Ardeshir Dady in 1810, the business for the "Commanders of India-men-of-war" has been carried on by Curshedji and Jehangir Ardeshir (sons of the late Ardeshir) jointly with me, and since Mr. Milburn's arrival at this place, I recommended Curshedji and Jehangir Ardeshir strongly to him. Limji Cowasji my brother, who is managing under Curshedjee and Jehangir, acts at the same time for Mr. Milburn, and had lately the management for Captain Larkins of the Comoden, who had some quarrel with Limji and others, for the sale of some cotton goods. I was requested to interfere in the matter, and succeeded to bring them to terms ; but since, they have given me to understand that they wish in future to act separately, and as Limji's transactions have lately caused my displeasure, I therefore intend to leave that concern, and believe, I shall do equally as well without them, and be free of all further blame. As to Curshedji and Jehangir Ardeshir—their grandfather and father were my particular friends, and assisted me a great deal in the commencement of my mercantile transactions in consequence I feel myself bound to do as much good to his sons as it lies in my power, without injury to myself.

In another letter to Thomas Price, Esq., dated 11th September 1822 Framji states as follows :—

> THOMAS PRICE, Esq.,
>   Richmond, Near London.

MY DEAR SIR,

Convinced of your good intentions to serve an old acquaintance of yours, to promote his views in a mercantile object. I shall venture to state here a few circumstances, which I hope will convince you that I deserve your friendly assistance. It will be well known to you that I have been concerned for many years in the transactions carried on by the sons of the late Ardeshir Dady (Curshedji and Jehangir Ardeshir) for the management of East Indiamen, which were chiefly recommended to them through my influence, and not only this, but the laborious task I undertook to settle deranged affairs of the late Ardeshir Dady, will be a proof that I wished to do as much good to the sons of my benefactor (Ardeshir Dady) as lay in my power.

From these two letters it will clearly be observed what were Framji's feelings towards his benefactors, and there are still many more expressions of the same sentiments towards them, but I shall be content with these only. It also shows that singular frankness and openness of heart, for which he was so remarkable. He had no artificial disguise or concealment to hide his motives ; but spoke out boldly and frankly whatever his sentiments were regardless to any one, adhering always to the truth. This was one of the most remarkable and conspicuous trait in his character.

It was not only so far back as 1822, that he expressed these sentiments towards his benefactors, but he bore the same sentiments of respect and gratitude up to the last moment of his life. Although a great family dissension arose between him in the latter days of his life, and the surviving members of that renowned family of Dady Sett, owing to some domestic disagreement, even then, he did not lower the estimation he had for them, but continued to speak of them with all respect and esteem and keeping in his mind the feelings of gratitude he owed to those noble Setts—Dady and Ardeshir—calling them always his benefactors.

Cowasji Byramji was the youngest son of Byramji Banaji Limji, familiarly known as Cowasji Goga. Mr. Cowasji commenced life by joining his father's firm known as the Banaji Limji, with his brothers and cousins. But owing to some dispute having arisen among the partners, he severed his connection with the firm in 1809, and opened a grand shop of English goods at Bazar Gate Street. Mr. Cowasji passed the latter part of his life rather solitarily, and died at an advanced age of 90, on 16th December 1834.

Having deviated much from the subject, I will now go back and trace the birth and early life of Mr. Framji in the next chapter.

CHAPTER II.

His parentage, early life and mercantile porpensities.

Framji, the eldest son of Cowasji Byramji Banaji, was born in Bombay, in his maternal grandfather's residence in Todd Street (Byramji Homji Street) within the Fort, on the 22nd day of 7th month of the year 1137 Yazdazard (Cudmee), *i.e.* 1767 A.D. From his father's side, he was a descendant of the Banaji family and from his mother's side that of the Dady Sett.

His parents were not in very affluent circumstances. His father possessed some small landed property, and lived respectably. Of Framji's early career very little is now known. But this much is certain, that from his very infancy he showed signs of his future greatness In those days, when education was of a low standard in Bombay, and men's minds were chiefly bent only on money making (for those are the days still calling fresh, in the memory of the old, as the good old times) it is scarcely possible to believe that Framji could have received the rudiments of a high education. He, however, went through the usual routine in those days, the education imparted in Mehtaji School (scarcely deserving the name of education). He commenced receiving the rudiments of education, at the age of seven, in the school of a Brahamin Mehtaji, by name Bapubhai Sobharam whom he greatly respected in his days of prosperity. Having remained there for nearly four years, he was then transferred at the age of eleven, to a higher school, the *Pantuji's Pathshalla*. At the age of twelve, he was put under the charge of Mr. La Ford to learn English. He was, indeed, by nature destined to be no insignificant a character, and it was by his own strong penetration and sound judgment, notwithstanding, the very crude education he must have received, he shone forth in the leading van of his country, and in his ideas of reformation in his own community, as well as the Indian communities in general, he shot far ahead of his age.

This trait of a naturally fertile genius, which would have much improved by a better and more sound education, cannot still be underrated,—far from what he has done, and left behind him for his community, nay more! for his country, it is obvious that he has done a great deal more than any other man of his time.

Notwithstanding, the sudden encomiums, by which the withdrawal of this great and good man, from the scene of life, in which he displayed a conspicuous part, may have been followed, and the condemnation which malice might dictate, of which there is yet none, we do leave him to an impartial tribune in posterity, when all the presiding influences have passed away, to pass a calm and matured verdict, and no doubt they will pronounce him to be the most honest man who ever lived, a man who had the good of his country and countrymen at heart, and one who knew his duties towards them, and performed them satisfactorily and creditably.

It will be the height of presumption in me, to call him the most perfect man, for whoever came upon the stage of this world, was never perfect, and so he was not,—there were in him his relative blemishes, but these instead of pointing out as marked defects, and overshadowing the picture, rather added lustre to the dazzling brilliancy of his career.

After receiving the then education of reading and writing Gujrati and English, at the age of twenty, Framji thought of launching into the world, and trying his chance as a merchant. He first started in life as a Dubash under his maternal uncle Dady Sett, who vastly traded with England and China. Having spent eight years as a Dubash, in the years 1796 and 1798 Framji twice went to China as an agent to Dady Sett in his own ship "The Shah Ardeshir." In these two trips to China, he acquired a vast knowledge of the different branches of trade, which proved very beneficial to his master. Before his return from the second trip to China, Dady Sett died, and Ardeshir Sett engaged him as his assistant, and chiefly kept him in Bombay.

In 1804 Ardeshir Sett gave Mr. Framji a small house in Todd Street in the Fort (the house in which he was born) at a very low price, and which he improved according to his own taste.

In the year 1801 Framji was employed as a Dubash to the East India Company's ships.

At the age of 38, in the year 1806, Framji threw off all yoke of dependence, and started in business at his own risk and responsibility. At the persuation of several merchant friends Framji in partnership with his brother Mr. Nusservanji bought in the year 1807 a ship called "Salamani," weighing 679 tons, from an Arab merchant by name Husan Abdulla, for Rs. 1,33,000, in which they exported cotton to China. On this occasion several other merchants had also sent to sea three vessels, by name "Asia," "James Drumond," and "Brunswick," for the port of China. At this time a war was raging on between the English and the French. Three of the vessels fell victim in the hands of the French, but "Salamani" which was a very speedy one, fortunately escaped and reached China safely. It so happened, that owing to this incident, the value of cotton went up so high in the mart of China, that the owners of the vessel as well as the merchants almost made a fortune. From this fortunate circumstance, both the brothers separated the partnership, and Framji carried on business on his own account. In the year 1811, Framji opened a branch at Calcutta, where he first sent his brother Mr. Byramji as his agent, from whence he was transferred to China, and Mr. Curshedji, the third brother, was sent to Calcutta. Thus one after the other, Mr. Navroji, Mr. Rustomji and Mr. Limji, together with the other three abovenamed brothers, were sent by Framji, as his agents to Calcutta and China by turns. All of these six brothers owe their rise to their eldest brother Framji.

Framji's trade was not only limited to China and Calcutta, but extended over Madras, England and many other places. In all Framji was master of six large vessels, viz., "Salamani," "Minerva," "Bombay Castle," "Golconda," "Buckinghamshire," and "Sharah." In the year 1819 Framji sold his firm at Calcutta to his younger brother Mr. Rustomji Cowasji, who henceforth carried on extensive trade on that side, and was reckoned amongst one of the millionaires of the time.

CHAPTER III.

Framji's brothers and their career.

Here I think it will not be out of place to give a short sketch of the career of Framji's younger brothers, who, though owed their rise to him, have left a good name behind them.

Nusservanji Cowasji Banaji was the second son of Cowasji Behramji Banaji. From the very beginning he worked in partnership with his elder brother, Framji, and had through him gone to China also. In 1811, he severed his partnership and carried on his own business. He died at an early age of 42, on the 9th December 1818.

Navrosji Cowasji Banaji was the third son of Cowasji Behramji Banaji. He also commenced life as a partner in the firm of his elder brother, Framji, and in 1808 had gone to China, as his agent. After remaining for about four years in China, he came to Calcutta in 1812, where he carried on his own business. He died at the early age of 41, on the 7th February 1819.

Behramji Cowasji Banaji was the fourth son of Cowasji Behramji Banaji. In the beginning, he joined his eldest brother, Framji, in business, but soon after carried on at his own account an extensive trade with Calcutta and China. He owned a grand vessel called "John Bannerman," built after his own style and model of invention at Surat, and had also two smaller ones. On the 28th of June 1830, he took from the Government the village of Anik, on a yearly rental of Rs. 800, and had greatly enhanced its value by cultivating the land. After his death, the Government handed over the village to his family for Rs. 10,000, but in 1837 it was purchased by the late Framji Nusservanji Patel. Behramji was familiarly known by the name of " *Behramji Amba.*" In 1824 he sank several wells in different parts of the city of Bombay, owing to the then great scarcity of water. He, in the later part of his life, used to import Arab horses from Arabia and had a big stable at Bhendy Bazar, but this business did not prove profitable. He was among the foremost of his enlightened countrymen, the Parsees, to whose general enterprise and liberality, he added the ingenuity of a European artist, and the manly frankness of European manners. During the greater part of his career, his munificence and charity were as large as his fortune ; and though in the autumn of his life misfortune overtook him, and a princely estate, fell like his years, " into the seir and yellow leaf," his generosity, and independence of character never forsook him ; he died even more honored and more beloved in poverty, than he had been in wealth, a rare and unerring test of genuine worth. He died at the age of 53, on the 3rd December 1833.

Limji Cowasji Banaji was the fifth son of Cowasji Behramji Banaji. He first joined in business with his father-in-law, Mr. Ardeshir Dady Sett, and after his death in 1810, Limji carried on his own business, and was a broker to Messrs. Rimington and Crawford, Messrs. Milburn & Co., and Messrs. Adam Sikner. He died at the comparatively early age of 45, on the 7th June 1828.

Curshedji Cowasji Banaji was the sixth son of Cowasji Behramji Banaji. He first did the petty business of a Dubash, but afterwards joined his brother, Framji, in business. On the death of his brother Limji, he was appointed broker to Messrs. Remington & Co. In 1838, he opened his own firm called " Curshedji Cowasji & Co." in partnership with Messrs. Framjee Pestonji Patak and Muncherji Framji Cama, and carried on an extensive trade

with England, China and Calcutta. In 1842, he took over
the firm to himself and called it " Messrs Curshedji Cowasji
and Sons." He owned six large vessels, called " Ardeshir,"
" Charles Grant," " Castle Huntley," " Kandhar," " Captain
Herbert," and "Pearl." He was the owner of the large building at Colaba known as the " Grant Buildings." In 1830,
he received from Government seven villages in the island of
Salsett, on a yearly rental of Rs. 2,708, but as he greatly
improved the land, the Government handed him over those
villages for the sum of Rs. 30,000 on the 23rd September
1843. He was nominated one of the first twelve Justices of
Peace in 1834, and was a leading member on the Board of
the Parsee Panchayat. He was a man of sterling probity
and uprightness, of great liberality and kindness of disposition, and of an evenness of temper, scarcely capable
of being disturbed. He was well known to nearly the
whole of the European community, and respected wherever
he was known. His enlarged heart and liberal hand
recognised no distinction of colour or of creed, but were
ever open as day to melting charity, and accessible to all
who had suffering or misfortune, on which to found their
claims. His demise was of universal regret, which took
place on the 4th of December 1847.

Rustomji Cowasji Banaji, the youngest son of Cowasji
Behramji Banaji, entered his eldest brother, Framji's business in 1807, and first travelled over to Calcutta in the year
1812. From thence he went over twice to China, and once
to Madras and Ceylon, and returning from his travels
in 1817, he settled for good in Calcutta. He first joined
his brother, Navrosji, in business at Calcutta, but after his
death in 1819, opened his own firm in the name and style
of Messrs. Rustomji Turner & Co., in partnership with Mr.
Robert Turner. In 1827, he opened a branch office at China,
in the name of his two sons, Maneckji and Dadabhoy Rus-

tomji. He with several other leading merchants of Calcutta bought a big dock at Kiderpore, belonging to Mr. James Kid, for Rs. 3,51,000, and also another known as " Shalkia Dock " belonging to Messrs Curry and Co., for Rs. 2,00,000 and under his Secretary-ship was opened the " Calcutta Docking Company " in 1837 ; he also established the first insurance company called the " Sim Insurance Company " in 1834. He was the owner of no less than twenty-seven big vessels, fifteen of which were chartered for Rs. 1,15,000 a year by the British Government during the first Chinese War. He had further opened the first " Cotton Pressing Factory," and also a " Paper Manufacturing Company " in Calcutta.

In 1838 he called over his whole family to Calcutta and the ladies of his family were the first to cross the seas over to Calcutta. Writing on this subject the *Bombay Gazette* of the 16th July 1838 says :—" Our Parsee friends who have so long been foremost among the natives of this country in everything connected with commercial enterprise, are now about to set an example in what may at first sight be considered a purely domestic matter, but which will in all probability in its ulterior results from throwing aside the trammels of ancient prejudices, be productive of singular changes. The Lady of Rustomji Cowasji, Esq., the distinguished and liberal minded merchant in Calcutta, is about to sail from Bombay for that port, in a few days, accompanied by the wife of his son and a Cortege of female attendants—to those who remember that but a few years ago no Parsee female of respectability would proceed even to the Deccan, the contemplated trip of these fair voyagers will afford much food for speculation upon the rapid change which the march of opinion has effected."

In 1839 he built a small Fire-temple for the use of his community. He had reside l for over thirty years in Calcutta, and for a greater part of that time, carried on a very extensive business as a merchant and shipowner, and for his activity and enterprise was well known to men of business all over the East. During his prosperity, he sought European society and breaking through the restraints, usual among his countrymen, did not hesitate to introduce the ladies of his family to his guests, among whom the Governor General of India had more than once been present. Rustomji was extremely liberal, while he had the means, and there might be many yet, who have felt his kindness, when it was of the utmost value to them. He died on the 15th April 1852, at the age of 60.

CHAPTER IV.

Framji's connection with the Elphinstone Institute and the Parsee Panchayat. How he supported native education.

Not only did Framji make a name in his mercantile capacity, but also in the advancement and improvement in the social condition of his countrymen. He was a man, who never sought for honour, but was one of those, who are sought for being honoured. Through his influence, he got into employment all his brothers and relatives, and was ever ready to do all, he can to relieve and redress the grievances of the poor. Though engaged so deeply, he did not neglect for a moment the welfare of his country and countrymen.

The public measure of the greatest utility, with which Framji's name is closely associated, is—the early advocacy of the cause of native education in this island, not only male education, but also female education, at a time when there was scarcely one to be found amongst us, who could openly declare himself in favour of it.

What Framji has done in the cause of native education, has, I believe, been so eminently recorded on the files of the Elphinstone Institution, of which he was not only an original member, but a staunch supporter, and one of the few, who took the initiative in its formation. The same may be said as regards the Grant Medical College, the Native Public Dispensary, the Agri-Horticultural Society, and many others. In short, in his days of power, he stood foremost in his evertions, and unsparing in his purse in the furtherance of objects calculated to benefit his fellow-beings.

In the year 1820 Framji was appointed a member on the board of " Native School Book and School Society."

Under the presidency of the Rt. Hon'ble Mountstuart Elphinstone, the Governor of Bombay, and the Secretary-ship of Capt. Jarvis, Framji in the year 1827 opened the first Anglo-Gujrati School, under the name of " The Native Education Society." Framji was appointed a member of the Board of Directors, which honour he enjoyed for a period of twenty-eight years, and which he resigned only seven months prior to his death. When Mr. Liget, the President of the Board, together with the Chief Justice the Hon'ble Sir Askin Pery, and the Hon'ble Mr. Jugunath Sunkersett, sent an application to H. E. the Governor of Bombay, for the approval of the appointment of Mr. Bomanji Hormasji Wadia, in place of the deceased gentle-man, with words of estimation for his past services, the Secretary to H. E. the Governor wrote as follows :—

" I have been directed to inform you that the honour which the Board have paid to the late Mr Framji Cowasji Banaji is thoroughly worthy of the memory of the deceased. His Excellency and the Council themselves, together with those who have gone before them, have expressed their highest opinion about the merits of this honoured gentle-man, and the very same opinion is still entertained. Pro-moting the advancement of one's own country is serving right his country was the idea of this gentleman, and in accordance to it he has acted, and so we all appreciate the worth of so good a gentleman."

From the time when the genius of the Rt. Hon'ble Mountstuart Elphinstone sought to invite the upper class of Natives to measures for the introduction of National Eductation, Framji Cowasji was distinguished as the most active promoter of this object. He was an original mem-ber of the well-known Elphinstone Institute, which he joined in 1835, and until advancing years and increasing infirmities induced him to retire, was year after year elected by his countrymen to represent them at the Board of Education. He was the first Parsee gentleman who educated the females of his family. As already noticed Framji was a great enthusiast in the cause of Native Education, both male and female. It was his opinion that education should be given to every person according to his abilities and means. He had very liberal views on the subject of Female education, and notwithstanding the strong opposition from every quarter, he set on foot instructing his daughters and grand-daughters in English. His efforts at the time proved unsuccessful, but later on they were matured. He had even independently of the strong opposition from his country-men, publicly declared in his capacity of a Member of the Board of Education, his opinion in favour of female education, and set the noble example in his own family circle.

Framji contributed the sum of Rs. 10,000 towards the maintenance and support of the "Native Education Society," and also gave large sums of money for establishing professorships at the Elphinstone Institution.

Framji was the first among the Natives, who boldly came forward as an advocate for firmly establishing the rights and claims of the Natives upon Government, and warmly discussing the then topic of making Natives eligible for members of the " Grand Jury " and other officers of trust and responsibility under Government. He headed the list of the requisition sent in to the House of Commons, through Sir Charles Forbes, on 31st December 1829, asking for the admission of Natives to the Grand Jury, and for making them Justices of Peace, and also give them high and responsible posts under the Government and for the improving of justice in the Mofussil.

Framji was one of twelve Natives, namely :—Messrs. Jamsetji Jeejibhoy, Navrosji Jamshedji Wadia, Bomanji

Hormusji Wadia, Curshedji Cowasji Banaji, Curshedji Ardeshir Dady, Dadabhoy Pestonji Wadia, Hormusji Bhicaji
Chinoy, Curshedji Rustomji Wadia, Juggunath Sunkersett,
Dhakji Dadaji, Mohmudally Roghey, and Mohmud Ibrahim
Mueba, who first held the Commission of the Peace in the
year 1834, and those who have set on the Bench with him,
remember the independence, and impartiality, with which
he administered justice.

On the 11th of July 1836 Framji, in co-operation with
Sir Jamsetji Jeejibhoy and Jeejibhoy Dadabhoy, opened a
school, for the religious training of the youths of his community called the " Zand School " for which he contributed
the sum of Rs. 3,000

In 1841 Framji was elected a member of the Board of
Education.

The Parsees, as a distinct community, looked up to him
as their leader, who was ever ready to render his services
for the general good of the community, and his exertions
for introducing—various reforms in his own community, in
his capacity of a leading member of the Parsee Panchayat.

Framji was likewise the foremost in bringing about the
Parsee Panchayat once more into existence, and was elected
a member of that Institution on the 4th of March 1818, and
was in 1821 nominated a Trustee of its Funds. As a member
of the Parsee Panchayat, Framji exercised so beneficial an
influence over the morals of the Parsee community, that
the records of that old and once respected Institution are
stamped with many tokens of his strong sense and excellent
judgment.

The Parsee Panchayat exercised for a time a sovereign
power, and was a tribunal for the settlement of all social
and matrimonial questions among Parsees; but afterwards,
instead of directing their labours and energies to a right

end, had much abused their power, when Framji in disgust tendered his resignation along with Mr. Nowrosji Jamsetji Wadia in the year 1836, passing a very strong censure on the mismanagement of that body. A correspondent under the *nom de plume* Q in the Corner contributes to the *Bombay Times* of 1845 an English translation of Mr. Framji's minute which is as follows :—Framji says :—" I have resigned from the Board of the Parsee Panchayat along with Mr. Navroji Jamshedji Wadia, and if I were to enumerate the reasons for my so doing, it would fill up a big volume. For some time past, we have failed in bringing about profitable arrangements in our community, and to speak more plainly, we have rather done evil than any good. Various evils have creeped into our community and many are the bad results arising from them, and I do not think it advisable to dwell at length upon those. There are at present many instances of forsaking one's own wife and residing with another and of taking into the Zorastrian religion children born of kept mistresses. The Panchayat seems to take no notice of such evil-doers nor punish them, but they freely join with us in the Gumbhar feasts and even enter the sacred precincts of our fire-temples. The past dread has gone, because the Panchayat does not take them to task. Consequently such crimes daily increase, and I think that within ten or twenty years henceforth, the ladies of our community will come forward to dance in public as those of Hindoos and Mahomedans. It is a matter of great regret that in such advanced times we could not check such crimes, nor give impartial justice to the aggrieved. The main cause of this is that there is discord and disunion amongst ourselves, the leaders of the community. In short, I must say again that we are rather doing evil than any good, and we will be responsible for the same before the Almighty. All this disorder and miscarriage is owing to the want of union amongst us. We had the means to stop these evils but we did not use them."

The next year a reconciliation was brought about, and both these gentlemen rejoined the Parsee Panchayat, but since then, it has been dwindling into almost a defunct body.

Framji ever displayed in a remarkable degree that characteristic and genuine warmth of feeling, of an honest mind, one who deeply felt for his fellow-beings, and wanted to do them as much good as it lay in his power.

There are several records of the late Parsee Panchayat, illustrative of the depth of penetration and a true love for his country and countrymen, which he possessed in no small a degree. He deserves still a higher credit than this, for the very object of which in the present state of the Parsee community, the society called " The Rahanumahe Mazdiashna Sabha "—a guide to the followers of Mazdiashna religion—is brought into existence, occupied his thoughts all the while, and he had to a very great extent effected the very reforms, which they have now introduced, and would have even so far succeeded to bring about a complete reformation, as to leave a permanent effect on the Parsee mind, but he failed in that laudable effort, owing to the discord and disunion, which then prevailed among his other colleagues in the Panchayat.

Notwithstanding the sterling virtues in Framji's character, there was a weak point to be marked in it, that often times the kindness and benevolence of his disposition prevailed over strict and firm resolution. Great men are often not without peculiar defects, which they cannot see for themselves, for no man can clearly point out all his faults; and under the influence, of these they sometimes fall into very serious mistakes, which it is impossible for them to rectify afterwards, and there are a few only who, when their mistakes are clearly pointed out to them, do acknowledge their faults and repent for them; but there are also some, who under these circumstances, still persist in maintaining their wrong and erroneous opinions, notwithstanding the clear way in which their faults are brought home to them. This distinguished man, of whom I am speaking, was not of the latter sort, for when his faults were pointed out to him, he on being convinced, readily acknowledged them and tried as far as possible in future to keep aloof from them. Notwithstanding his own precautions, he was often entrapped in the snares of disguise, conceit, and cunning of others. This simplicity of a kind disposition was often worked upon by other enticing persons to serve their own peculiar ends; for the true frankness of his heart and the openness of his mind never for a moment doubted the motives or objects of others, though many a time he fell a victim to their deceit. Another admirable and peculiar feature in his character consisted in his too kind and forgiving a disposition. He was ever confident in others—that is, placed too much reliance in his dealings with others—and when he came to understand that they betrayed the trust reposed in them, he had no other recourse but to blame himself for it.

CHAPTER V.

Loss of his son Edulji.   Suppyling water to the Two Tanks,
from Moogbhat Oart.

On the 3rd of April 1824, Edalji, the second son of
Framji, while returning on foot from Madras, died at the
age of 30, at the village of Chock, about eight miles from
Panwal, by the accidental bursting of a rifle. Framji, to
perpetuate the memory of his beloved son, did a very noble
act of charity, which has handed down his name to posterity.
At the time we are speaking of, there was a great scarcity
of water, and the inhabitants of Kamateepoora, Grant Road
and Girgaum, had to go about from place to place in search
of water.   Framji took to heart their want, and remedied
the evil.   He bought the spacious ground, called the Moogbhat Wadi, opposite the Cowasji Patel's Tank, and there
sank three big wells, from which through water pipes (at a
time when such a thing was but a novelty) he carried water
by means of steam-engines and cattle-wheels to the Two Tanks
at Kamateepoora.   On this he is said to have spent more
than thirty thousand rupees, and moreover maintained it at
a monthly cost of Rs. 200.   He carried on this maintenance
till the year 1831, when thinking, that his descendants
should perhaps fail to carry on this work of charity, he, in
the month of October of the same year, wrote to Mr.
Charles Norris, the Chief Secretary to the Bombay Government, saying that he had spent over a lack and a half for the
improvement of his Poway estate, for which he had to pay
to the Government the sum of Rs. 4,797-2-0 every year,
and that neither he nor his descendants had any hope of
recovering the amount already spent ; he therefore requested the Government to hand over that estate to him as a

free-hold, on payment of Rs. 46,000, and that during his life-time. he would carry on supplying water to the Two Tanks and that after his death, he would set aside a yearly income of Rs. 2,400 from his Poway estate for the maintenance of the same. Writing on the subject to the Government, Framji says :—"I beg to state that from a charitable motive I was led, many years ago, to sink wells for the better and constant supply of fresh water from my Oart called Moogbhat, through the aqueduct of the two reservoirs situated on the (new town) Duncan Road, for the use of the inhabitants of Kamateepoora. For the purpose, I obtained every assistance from Major Dickinson, and by his advice sank three wells in the said Oart, Moogbhat, and set up a steam engine and four wheels with cattle to draw water, the whole of which work was not completed under an outlay of about Rupees thirty thousand, in addition to which, I have, all along, maintained an establishment at a monthly charge of about Rupees two hundred or Rupees two thousand and four hundred per annum. The supply of fresh water leads from the aforesaid Mooogbhat through aqueduct to the two Reservoirs erected on the Duncan Road, by the late Major Hawkins from the bequest of Uslaji, deceased. These reservoirs were delivered to my charge on the 7th May, 1825, by Major Bellasis, and ever since I have continued the supply of fresh water. The continuance of these useful works during my life-time in the same spirit, which first prompted me to undertake them, is certain, but without in any degree wishing to detract from the benevolent intentions of those who may succeed me, I may, I trust, be excused for expressing a desire for wishing to perpetuate them. Whatever may be the disposition of my heirs, I cannot reasonably expect that they should contribute thus materially to the public welfare without some consideration from a liberal and enlightened Government. Looking, therefore, to the importance of these works to the great and essential benefit resulting from them and to the desirableness of rendering them, as far as practicable, lasting, I cannot but entertain a lively hope that the proposition I am desirous of making toward accomplishing so important an object will, if coming within the bounds of reason and moderation, be received and viewed with that consideration and liberal attention which I am fully sensible it is the desire and wish of the Right Hon'ble the Governor in Council to extend towards all propositions of public utility emanating from the natives of the country.

" The Poway Estate, it will be remembered, was originally conferred on the late Doctor Scott, but resumed in conseqence of a failure on the part of his heirs or agents in paying the assessment of Government revenue ; impressed, therefore with the hopes to which my past exertions have given rise and with an anxiety to avoid any such failure on the part of my family, I beg to propose that instead of paying a yearly revenue of Rupees four thousand seven hundred and ninety-seven, two quarters and twenty-four reas, I hope I may be permitted to discharge the amount of ten years' purchase or Rupees forty-six thousand, the net amount, and henceforward to hold it as Free Hold Estate, and a deed may be made by the Government, to be continued to me and my heirs, and further, I would beg to propose on the expiration of the forty years rent free Lease, under which I held the waste land connected with the Estate and the rent on the same may be fixed, and my heirs may be permitted to redeem it in like manner by payment of the amount of ten years' purchase. The proposal made by me, which is under the expectation to a perpetual and permanent provision in order to continue the supply of fresh water from my charitable Oart called Moogbhat, through the acqueducts to those Reservoirs built by the late Major

Hawkins from the bequest of the said Uslajee, I intend to insert in my last Will and Testament about the charitable object in the manner as follows :—That my children may receive the revenue from my Poway Estate on Salsette and out of which is to defray the expense for the establishment kept at the charitable Oart, Moogbhat, and in default thereof I intend to empower the Right Honorable the Governor in Council that they will compell on my heirs, if the supply of water will be neglected to continue for ever from my said Oart, Moogbhat, and an expense for the said establishment to be paid from the collection of the revenue of my Poway Estate on Salsette."

In reply to this Mr. Williams, the Secretary to the Bombay Government, wrote to Mr. Framji on the 16th November 1831 :—

" In reply I am desired to acquaint you that observing with great satisfaction your exertions for the extension of cultivation and general improvement of Salsette and appreciating the Public spirit you have manifested and the charitable motives which prompt you to perpetuate so great a benefit to the inhabitants of the populous districts in which the reservoirs are situated as that which they now enjoy, through your memo. The Right Honorable the Governor in Council will have much pleasure in bringing your application to the favourable notice of the Honourable Court of Directors, with a strong recommendation from this Government that your request may be complied with."

On the 28th of October 1835, the Court of Directors sent the following despatch complying with Mr. Framji's request :—

" With respect to the proposal of Framji to purchase the Poway Estate which has been already granted to him in perpetuity, a proposal which he appears to have made with a laudable intention of providing for ever a supply of fresh water for the public reservoirs on the Duncan Road in the new town, we are disposed, as a special case, to accede to his request on the terms he has offered, namely, to pay a sum equal to ten years' purchase of the Estate, which on the annual rental (Rupees four thousand seven hundred and forty-seven) will amount to Rupees forty seven thousand four hundred and seventy."

Thus the supply of fresh water to the Two Tanks from Framji's charitable Oart, Moogbhat, was carried on till recently by his descendants. The following is the tablet on one of the Two Tanks at Duncan Road.—

THE WELLS

FROM WHICH THESE RESERVOIRS ARE SUPPLIED,

and the Establishment for drawing the water are maintained

By FRAMJEE COWASJEE,

In commemoration of whose Liberality

THIS TABLET IS PLACED BY THE BRITISH GOVERNMENT.

CHAPTER VI.

The grant of the Poway Estate.

The East India Company had in the year 1799 A. D. granted to an old British Officer, Surgeon Hellins Scott, several villages in the island of Salsette on a yearly rental of Rs. 3,200-4-0. Surgeon Scott enjoyed the income of these villages till the year 1816, when he went home and died there shortly after. As the descendents of Surgeon Scott could not continue paying the amount, in the year 1826 Mr. Simmonds, the Collector of North Concon, resumed the possession of those villages. Framji Cowasji sent in an application to the Government of Bombay on the 11th June 1829, asking to have those villages transferred to him on the same conditions as those with Surgeon Scott. In reply to this application, the Bombay Government through Mr. George Gilber, the then Collector of Concon, on the 15th of the same month, offered those villages to Mr. Framji, on a yearly rental of Rs. 4,001, and the following conditions :—

" You will promote the happiness and prosperity of the Ryots, and erect buildings, sink tanks, and wells, build embankments of fields and introduce the cultivation of superior articles of produce and extend the present culti-vation. Should you not attempt any of the improvements above mentioned within the period of ten years, the Govern-ment is at liberty to resume the grant within the period of ten years, should you expend capital in buildings, &c., as above the grant of the villages and lands will be considered confirmed to your Heirs and Assigns, &c., in perpetuity. You will make annual reports to the Hoozoor of whatever improvements you have made during the preceding year; the Collector will inspect and cause entries of the same to be recorded in the Duftur, you are not at liberty to dispose of in any way the above property to any other persons within the period of ten years.

You will receive the same rates of assessment as at present in force and no more and introduce no innovation in the particular without express sanction.

The Abkari has been included in the lease given to you. You are at liberty to sell liquor to the Ryots of your Estate only, and not to the other contractors without first obtaining permission of the Collector. If any farmer or contractor requires liquor, he must make application to the Sirkar, and permission shall be granted in the event of there being a general scarcity of this commodity, in the other parts of the Salsette Prant, should you export it beyond the limits of Salsette Talooka, you will pay the established export fee, besides you must adhere to the Rules established, and to be established with the liquor contractors in Salsette.

You will continue the Davustans, Dharmadaes and Paldars as at present."

After this on the 20th of November 1829, Framji applied for a grant of the two adjoining villages of Toongwy and Puspolie. These two villages were also granted to Mr. Framji on the 22nd March 1830 on a yearly rental of Rs. 1,787, and on the following conditions :—

" You are properly to protect the Ryots of the villages and to execute the undermentioned works therein. In the Village of Toongwy, you are to build and repair Tanks, and to build a Dhurmsala, and to sink in the waste lands as many Wells, as may be required, to bring them into cultivation. In the Village of Puspolie, you are to sink ten Wells of stone and mortar at the rate of one Well per annum for the irrigation of the waste lands, you are to prepare the Tanks, Dhurmasala and Wells as above and by every means to introduce valuable products into the villages, or in failure of doing so to assign satisfactory reason to Government."

On the 5th of July 1830 the Government through Mr. Boyd, the then Collector, made a reduction of Rs. 990, for waste lands and thereby fixed the yearly assessment on the seven villages at Rs. 4,797-9-0.

In appreciation of Framji's public spirit, and the charitable motives which ever prompted him to redress and remedy the grievances of his fellow beings, the Court of Directors, as stated in the preceding pages, handed over the Poway Estate, including Poway and the seven adjoining villages, to Framji as a Free-hold estate on payment of a sum of Rs. 47,470 on the 15th of February 1837. The following is the deed by which the " East India Company " transferred to Framji the sole right of the Poway Estate :—

" 𝕿𝖍𝖎𝖘 𝕴𝖓𝖉𝖊𝖓𝖙𝖚𝖗𝖊, made the Fifteenth day of February in the year of Christ one thousand Eight hundred and thirty-seven Between the Honorable East India Company of the one part and Framji Cowasji Banaji Esquire of Bombay Parsee Merchant of the other part. WHEREAS by a Deed bearing date the thirteenth day of August one thousand seven hundred and ninety-nine purporting to be a grant to Helenus Scott had been for some time therein described as Surgeon in the service of the United Company of Merchants of England trading to the East Indies after Reciting therein that the said Helenus Scott had been for some time and was then in allowed possession of certain spot or parcels of ground situate in the limits of the Villages of Poway, Terandaz Comprey, Pospowly and Chandowley, included in the district of Marole Coorlim

and Moolly and in that of Trombay in the Island of Salsette
which spots or parcels of ground were the Property of the
said Company. It is declared that the said Company did
thereby unalienably grant and make over to the said
Helenus Scott, his Heirs, Executors Administrators and Assigns, all and sundry the aforesaid parcels or spots of ground
situated in the said Villages with a temporary exception
only in respect to certain spots of Serotore Tenure, which
were not to become his until he could satisfy and buy out
the then incumbents and subject to an annual payment of
the sum of three thousand and two hundred Rupees, three
quarters, and twelve reas, which was declared to be the
settled quit rent of the above grounds, on their reduced
assessments and it was thereby further agreed and determined upon by and between the said parties thereto that
if the said Helenus Scott, his Heirs, Executors, Administrators and Assigns, should fail to pay and make good all or
any part of the aforesaid assessment or quit rent in manner
therein mentioned within one month of the time therein
specified the Collector or other revenue officer for the time
being of Salsette, was thereby authorized to seize, or sell
any part of the aforesaid ground, or the tenements or
buildings, which might be thereon erected or the materials
which might thereto belong, in order to satisfy and make
good the amount of the said assessments or quit rent which
might then be due and owing. And it was thereby further
declared and agreed that WHEREAS over and above the
assessment on the above granted parcels of land or spots
of ground the Honorable Company had exercised and then
exercised a right of taxing certain Brab Trees growing
thereon at different rates according to their produce or
situation; and that the said Helenus Scott by felling of
wood, and draining of lands had brought forward with
much labour and expense, a considerable part of the grounds

included in the above grants into a state of great cultivation and consequent productiveness the said Company thereby relinquished all Property in the Brab or other Trees situated on any of the said lands and the said Trees, and such trees as might be produced thereafter were thereby declared and acknowledged to be the sole property of the said Helenus Scott, his Heirs, Executors, Administrators and Assigns AND WHEREAS the said Helenus Scott continued in possession of the said Estate and duly paid the said rent so received as aforesaid up to and until some time in or about the year one thousand eight hundred and sixteen when he proceeded to England where he afterwards departed this life and no further payment on account of the said rents was thereafter made by the said Helenus Scott or by his Heirs or by any person or persons on his behalf, AND WHEREAS James Bruce Simson, Esquire, as Collector of the Northern Concan some time in the year one thousand Eight hundred and twenty-six in consequence of the large amount of arrears of such rent then due and owing to the said Company, entered into and upon and seized and took possession of the said Estate and Villages and of all the Buildings and other Property thereon and continued in possession thereof on behalf of the said Company AND WHEREAS the said Framji Cowasji in a letter bearing date the Eleventh day of June one thousand Eight hundred and twenty-nine addressed to William Newnham, Esquire, Secretary to Government, stated as follows. I beg leave to propose to the Honorable the Governor in Council to take on a Lease for Ever the land of Poway, situated at Salsette near Bhandock (which was formerly held and occupied by late Doctor Scott declared on the following terms, that is to say upon paying annually the amount of present Revenue to the Government which is to the extent of Rupees Three thousand five hundred and nine, two quarters

and eighty eight reas, including of the Thoka on the Paddy
field at the rate of twenty Rupees per a Moora and all the
Grass and waste land appertaining thereto together with all
the trees of every description to be allowed me free from paying any kind of Tax whatsoever as in the same privilege and
manner as was granted to Do ctor Scott, I also beg leave to
state for the information of the Honorable the Governor in
Council that the said Poway Village from its situation now
appears to be in a ruined state in consequence of which it will
be necessary to put it in proper order, and for the improvement of the said Village requires a large sum of money all
which I will do myself, I therefore beg leave to request that
the Honorable the Governor in Council will be pleased to
take my proposal into his serious consideration and should
he think it proper to let it out upon the same terms and
conditions as it was formerly granted to Doctor Scott I am
under such supposition willing to become in occupation of
that Village for Ever and Ever, and a regular lease will be
duly executed AND WHEREAS by a certain instrument in
writing called a Cowl bearing date Soor Sun Sullaseen
Myalen Vu aleef A. D. One thousand Eight hundred and
twenty-nine and thirty (1829-30) Shuck one thousand seven
hundred and fifty-one (1751) Nerody nam Sumvuseer
purporting to be granted by George Gilberne, Esq., Collector of the Northern Concan to the said Framji Cowasji
therein described as Framji Cowasji Merchant of Bombay
it is stated as follows. You having preferred an application
in the English language dated the Eleventh day of June
one thousand eight hundred and twenty-nine, soliciting certain Villages and lands situated in the Turuf Marole Talook
Salsette and known by the name of Poway Estate on the
same terms as the same was granted to Doctor Scott with a
request to include the Abkaree the amount to be paid for
which to be regulated according to its average receipts for

several years. I reported on the subject on the Twenty-ninth day of the same month and received orders dated the Tenth and fifteenth day of July following to transfer the Villages and lands &c., according to the fixed boundaries of the Estate to you on lease. The following constitues the Estate, Mowja Poway, 2 Copre Coorah, 3 Terenda Lands, 4 Lands in the Mowza Puspowlee, 5 Mowza Sankee, 6 certain Brab Trees in the Mowza Vukerolee. The above has accordingly been given to you on lease from the current year Sun Sullasee A. D. One thousand eight hundred and twenty-nine and thirty (1829-30) on the conditions hereinafter provided for and in and by the said Cowl after setting forth therein the revenue which is thereby calculated to amount in the whole to four thousand and one Rupees on account of Villages and lands and Abkaree, to be paid annually into the Treasury of the Salsette Talook, on the First day of April in every year, the said Cowl proceeds as follows, Second you will promote the happiness and prosperity of the Ryots, and erect buildings, sink tanks and wells, build embankment of fields and introduce the cultivation of superior articles of produce and extend the present cultivation. Should you not attempt any of the improvements above mentioned within the period of Ten years the Government is at liberty to resume the grant within the period of Ten years, should you expend capital in buildings &c., as above the grant of the Villages and lands will be considered confirmed to you and to your Heirs and Assigns &c., in perpetuity. You will make annual reports to the Hoozoor of whatever improvements you have made during the preceding year the Collector will inspect and cause entries of the same to be recorded in the Dufter, you are not at liberty to dispose of in any way the above property to any other persons within the period of Ten years. Third you will receive the same rates of Assessment as at present in force and no more and introduce no innovation in the particular without express sanction. Fourth. The Abkaree has been included in the lease given to you. You are at liberty to sell Liquor to the Ryots of your Estate only and not to the other contractors without first obtaining permission of the Collector. If any farmer or contractor requires liquor he must make application to the Sirkar and permission shall be granted in the event of there being a general scarcity of this commodity, in the other parts of the Salsette Prant. Should you export it beyond the limits of the Salsette Talook, you will pay the Established export fee, besides you must adhere to the Rules established and to be established with the Liquor contractors in Salsette. Fifth. You will continue the Davustans, Dhurmadaes and Paldors as at present. AND WHEREAS, by a certain other instrument in wirting bearing date the Fifth day of July One thousand Eight hundred and thirty purporting to be additional clauses, it is stated amongst other things as follows : First. In the amount of Lease of the Poway Estate the Assessment of the waste land has been included in this subject. Mr. Boyd, the Collector, wrote to Government on the Eighteenth day of February One thousand Eight hundred and thirty, and procured an order dated the twenty-second day of March of the same year that this Assessment on the waste should be deducted from the amount of the Lease as was the case in the lease of the Villages Veyar and others of Turuf Marolee granted by Mr. Langford, Assistant Collector in charge, to Merwanjee Rustomjee in conformity to this order Rupees Nine hundred and ninety, one quarter and seventy-six reas should be deducted from the amount of the Lease Rupees Four thousand and one leaving Rupees three thousand and ten, two quarters and twenty-four reas which you are to pay annually and for which you will receive a receipt. Second. In order that the whole of the waste land in the aborementioned villages may be brought into cultivation a term of 40 years has been fixed during which no assessment will be levied thereon from the forty-first year after deducting the land totally incapable of cultivation the remainder whether culti- vated or waste will be assessed according to the usual rates and such assessment will be levied annually. You are moreover to bring one-fourth of the waste into cultivation in ten years from the date of this Lease. Third. The revenue of all Cowls of Mofee Istawa which have been granted in the above Villages is to be paid by you as it becomes due above the amount of your Lease. On the twentieth of November One thousand Eight hundred and twenty-nine you presented an English Petition in Bombay requesting a Lease of the Villages of Toongaye and Pushpolee of Turuf Marole Talooka Salsette which was reported upon on the Eighteenth day of February One thousand Eight hundred and thirty by Mr. Boyd and an order from Government was received dated the twenty-second day of March One thousand Eight hundred and thirty, directing the Villages to be granted to you. The villages are therefore leased to you as follows : The Village of Toongwy the whole Village of Puspolee of which certain lands were granted to you by the lease dated Fifth day of September One thousand Eight hundred and twenty-nine. Those two Villages have been granted to you in Lease from the current year One thousand Eight hundred and thirty-one, on the following terms and the said Instru- ment after stating the particulars of the Revenue including Abkaree of the said Villages which is thereby calculated to amount to Rupees one thousand and seven hundred, three quarters and forty eight reas proceeds as follows. This sum of seventeen hundred and eighty-seven Rupees you are to pay every year on or before the first day of April in the Currency receivable in the Salsette Treasury, in default of

which you will be proceeded against agreeably to the re-
gulations. You are properly to protect the Ryots of the
villages and to execute the undermentioned works therein. In
the Village Toongwy you are to build and repair the Tanks
and to build a Dhurmsala and to sink in the waste lands as
many Wells as may be required to bring them into cultivation
in the Village Puspolee you are to sink 10 Wells of stone
and mortar at the rate of one Well per annum for the irre-
gation of the waste lands you are to prepare the Tank Dhur-
amsala and Wells as above and by every means to introduce
valuable products into the villages or in failure of doing so
to assign satisfactory reason to Government should you fail
in any of these provisions within ten years from the date
of this Lease Government will be at liberty to resume the
Villages from you and you will be liable to a fine as far as
five hundred Rupees (500) for every Well not prepared according to agreement. Should you act up to the above condition the abovenamed Villages will be continued to you
and your Heirs in perpetuity you are to report annually to
the Collector the improvement you may have made in order
that that Officer may should he deem it necessary enquire
with them and record them in the office you are not permitted in any way to transfer these villages within ten years
you are to adhere in regard to these two villages to the after
mentioned clause of the Lease granted to you of the Poway
Estate of the fifth September One thousand eight hundred
and twenty-nine, Clauses, Third, fourth, fifth, seventh, eighth,
ninth and tenth. AND WHEREAS the said Instrument
after giving an account of the land population and Houses
of the villages thereby leased proceeds as follows. This
waste land is to be free of Assessment during forty years.
The Assessment will be levied from the forty-first year,
as stipulated in the second Additional Article and that
on land held under Cowls of Mafee Istowa as in the third

additional article. AND WHEREAS the said Framji Cowasji has since the date of the said Cowls expended large sums of money in improving the Land so granted to him and in complying with the conditions thereof and also in the erection of several large and commodious Bungalows in the Villages of Poway and Sankay also in the construction of Roads in digging and clearing out wells building and reparing Tanks and making other great and extensive improvements on the said Poway Estate and has thereby greatly contributed to the comfort, happiness and prosperity of the inhabitants of the aforesaid Villages AND WHEREAS the said Framji Cowasji in the month of October one thousand eight hundred and thirty-one wrote and forwarded to Charles Norris, Esq., the then Chief Secretary to Government a letter in which he stated as follows : I am induced to trespass on your attention for a short time to bring to the notice of the Right Hon'ble the Governor in Council the following circumstances and to entreat his indulgent consideration to the request which I most respectfully beg to prefer to enable me with more certainty to perpetuate my charitable intentions and to render my present humble efforts both more permanently and effectually beneficial to my Family. I beg to state that from a charitable motive I was led many years ago to sink wells for the better and constant supply of fresh water from my Oart called Moogbhat through the aqueduct of the two Reserviors situated on the (New Town) Duncan Road for the use of the Inhabitants of Camateepoora. For the purpose I obtained every assistance from Major Dickinson and by his advice sank three wells in the said Oart Moogbhat and set up a steam Engine and four wheels with cattle to draw water the whole of which work was not completed under an outlay of about Rupees thirty thousand in addition to which I have all along maintained an Establishment at a monthly charge

of about Rupees Two hundred or Rupees Two thousand
and four hundred per annum. The supply of fresh water
leads from the aforesaid Mugbhat through aqueduct to the
two Reserviors erected on the Duncan Road by the late
Major Hawkins from the bequest of Uslajee deceased.
These Reserviors were delivered to my charge on the
seventeenth day of May one thousand eight hundred and
twenty-five by Major Bellasis and ever since I have continued the supply of fresh water. The continuance of
these useful works during my life time in the same spirit
which first prompted me to undertake them is certain, but
without in any degree wishing to detract from the benevolent intentions of those who may succeed me, I may, I
trust, be excused for expressing a desire for wishing to
perpetuate them. Whatever may be the disposition of my
Heirs I cannot reasonably expect that they should contribute thus materially to the public welfare without some
consideration from a liberal and enlightened Government.
Looking therefore to the importance of these works to the
great and essential benefit resulting from them and to the
desirableness of rendering them as far as practicable lasting I cannot but entertain a lively hope that the proposition I am desirous of making towards accomplishing so
important an object will if coming within the bounds of
reason and moderation be received and viewed with that
consideration and liberal attention which I am fully sensible it is the desire and wish of the Right Hon'ble the
Governor in Council to extend towards all propositions of
public utility emanating from the Natives of the country.
Government has been pleased to grant me seven Villages
the chief of which is called Poway Estate on the Island of
Salsette, in my endeavours to improve which the accompanying substantial Translation of my Report to the Principal
Collector of the Konkan through the Komavesdar of Sal-

sette will I hope give the full information about the expenditure incurred during the two years it has been under my management the amount of which is nearly one and a half lac of Rupees I beg to observe that it is not my intention to limit my endeavours as regards the improvements I hope to be able to sink many more Wells but in those which have been already sunk I have been obliged to cut through the solid Rock twenty to thirty feet and even then experienced a scarcity of water during the month of April and May. Government having kindly directed me to be supplied with Boring Rods from Guncarriage manufactory I tried the experiment and got down as low as twenty feet, but some of the wells I was experienced with water. However, by the next April or May when the spring sinking down, I will try then again with the Boring Rods as low as to sixty or seventy feet, and when I have no doubt the lowest fountain will rise or flow up, but for the execution of this I have instructed my Agent in England to send me out a complete set of the best Boring Rods which I expect to receive very soon. Thus to forward the views of Government, for it was with such intention that the estate was originally conferred on me though I am free to confess not without sanguine hopes of benefitting myself or my children I have expended very near one and a half Lack of Rupees. But the result from such improvements and the general beneficial effects to be anticipated from them in the dissemination of a new spirit of enterprise throughout the country in the better cultivation of the Land in the introduction of new and superior articles of produce and in the general improvement of the cultivating classes, results to be reckoned upon from undertakings of such spirit and magnitude may form some claim on the liberality of Government. This Estate, it will be remembered, was originally conferred on the late Doctor Scott, but resumed in consequence of a failure on the part of his Heirs or Agents in paying the assessment of Government Revenue. Impressed therefore with the hopes to which my past exertions have given rise and with an anxiety to avoid any such failure on the part of my family I beg to propose that instead of paying a yearly revenue of Rupees Four thousand seven hundred and ninenty seven, two quarters and twenty-four reas I may be allowed to deduct, say, about two hundred Rupees as for a compensation for the ground used in cutting Roads to my Village as well as for the customary allowance to the Hereditary Offices as Patell and Mallaras of the said Village which was omitted to be inserted in the Lease executed of the said Village and after the deduction of the above sum it will remain about four thousand and six hundred Rupees or yearly to be paid by me which I hope I may be permitted at once to discharge the amount of ten years purchase or Rupees forty-six thousand, the net amount and henceforth to hold it as Free Estate and a Deed may be made by the Government to be continued to me and my Heirs and further I would beg to propose that on the expiration of the Forty years rent free Lease under which I held the waste land connected with the Estate and the rent on the same may be fixed and my heirs may be permitted to redeem it in like manner by payment of the amount of ten years purchase. The proposal made by me which is under the expectation to a perpetual and permanent provision in order to continue the supply of fresh water from my charitable Oart called Mugbhut through the aqueducts to those Reservoirs built by the late Major Hawkins from the bequest of the said Uslaji, I intend to insert in my last Will and Testament about the charitable object in the manner as following : That my children may receive the revenue from my Poway Estate on Salsette and out of which is to defray the expense for the establishment kept at the charitable Oart Mugbhat, and in default thereof I intend to empower the Right Honorable the Governor in Council that they will compell on my Heirs if the supply of water will be neglected to continue for ever from my said Oart Mugbhat and an expense for the said Establishment to be paid from the collection of the Revenue of my Poway Estate on Salsette. Should the Right Honorable the Governor in Council be graciously pleased to consider my request with a view to giving permanency to the charitable work alluded to in the first part of this letter as such as to encourage the efforts I have made and am still desirous of making to secure the consideration of Government I beg to assure him of the grateful and proud feeling with which the same will be for ever remembered. But if the Right Honorable the Governor in Council is unable to accede with my request without submitting it to the Honorable the Court of Directors I humbly solicit that they will be pleased to forward this to the favorable submission of the Honorable the Court of Directors. AND WHEREAS Mr. Williamson, the then Secretary to Government by his letter bearing date the sixteenth day of November One thousand Eight hundred and thirty-one addressed to the said Framji Cowasji was pleased to signify as follows :—" I am directed by the Right Honorable the Governor in Council to acknowledge the receipt of your letter to Mr. Chief Secretary Norris dated in last month soliciting that the Poway Estate may be made over to you and your Heirs in perpetuity on payment of the amount of Government Revenue for ten years as purchase money and stating that your principal object in preferring this request is to provide from a permanent source for the maintenance for ever of an establishment which has been kept up by you for some time past to supply with fresh water the Public Reservoirs on the Duncan Road. In reply I am desired to acquaint you that observing with great satisfaction your exertions for the extension of cultivation and general improvement of Salsette and appreciating the public spirit you have manifested and the charitable motives which prompt you to perpetuate so great a benefit to the inhabitants of the populous districts in which the reservoirs are situated as that which they now enjoy, through your memo. The Right Honorable the Governor in Conncil will have much pleasure in bringing your application to the favorable notice of the Honorable Court of Directors with a strong recommendation from this Government that your request may be complied with. AND WHEREAS the Right Honorable the Governor in Council having forwarded the application of the said Framji Cowasji to the Honorable the Court of Directors of the said East India Company the said Honorable Court by their letter bearing date the Twenty-eighth day of October one thousand eight hundred and thirty-five were pleased to signify as follows. With respect to the proposal of Framji to purchase the Poway Estate which has been already granted to him in perpetuity a proposal which he appears to have made with the laudable intention of providing for ever supply of fresh water for the public reservoirs on the Duncan Road in the new Town we are disposed as special case to accede to his request on the terms he has offered namely to pay a sum equal to ten years purchase of the Estate which on the annual rental (Rupees four thousand seven hundred and forty-seven) will amount to Rupees forty-seven thousand four hundred and seventy AND WHEREAS the said Framji Cowasji has requested that a Deed of conveyance may accordingly be executed to him granting the said Estate to him and His Heirs for ever which the Right Honorable the Governor in Council on behalf of the said Honorable Company has agreed to execute on his entering into a covenant to execute such Deed or other instrument as may be requisite to ensure his keeping up a supply of water for the inhabitants of the Duncan Road as aforesaid. NOW THIS INDENTURE WITNESSETH that in pursuance of the said agreement and for carrying the same into execution and also for and in consideration of the said sum of Forty-seven thousand four hundred and seventy Rupees of lawful current money of Bombay aforesaid by the said Framji Cowasji to the Honorable East India Company well and truly paid at or before the sealing and delivering of these presents the receipt whereof the said Company do hereby acknowledge and thereof and of and from every part thereof do Release, acquit and discharge the said Framji Cowasji his Heirs Executors Administrators and Assigns and every of them for ever by these presents they the said Company have granted, bargained, sold, released and confirmed and by these presents do grant, bargain, sell, release and confirm unto the said Framji Cowasji in his actual Possession and occupation now being all those adjacent Villages and lands as well inhabited as waste Lands as also cultivated and uncultivated Gardens Roads Paths Passages Tanks Wells buildings Erections Privileges and all and singular the appurtenances thereunto in any wise belonging described in the hereinbefore in part recited Cowls bearing date respectively the fifth day of September One thousand Eight hundred and twenty-nine and the fifth day of July one thousand eight hundred and thirty and denominated and being as follows that is to say All that village called Sankee containing by admeasurement three hundred Begas one quarter of a Bega and one Pond be the same little more or less all that other Village called Tonguy containing by admeasurement four hundred and thirty-six Begas three quarters of a Bega and three and a half Ponds be the same little more or less And that other Village called Kompree containing by admeasurement one hundred and

seventy-one Begas three quarters of a Bega and four Ponds
be the same little more or less all that other Village called
Poway containing by admeasurement six hundred and
eighty-two Begas two quarters of a Bega and three ponds
be the same little more or less. All that other Village
called Terundaz containing by admeasurement five hundred
and fifty-eight Begas one Pond and three quarters of a
Pond be the same little more or less And all that village
called Puspollee containing by admeasurement Eleven hundred and eighty-six Begas and three Ponds be the same
little more or less the description and boundaries whereof
are particularly inserted and delineated in and by the Map
or Plan of the Revenue survey of the Island of Salsette
dated in the year one thousand eight hundred and thirty
and deposited in the Office of the Collector of the Northern
Concan at Tannah on the Island of Salsette and are cir-
cumscribed and included by a line on the North by which
they are separated from the Lands belonging partly to the
village of Soy and partly to that of Veear on the South
partly by the Land of Mahole partly by that of Ghaut Kopur
partly by that of Chendowlie and partly by that of Merole
on the West partly by the Land of Murole and partly by that
of Moroshee and on the East partly by the Land of Hurreealy and partly by that of Kanjoor. Together with all the
Waste Land described in and by the aforesaid Cowl bearing
date the Fifth day of July one thousand eight hundred and
thirty and all other waste land of every description and all
and singular (Houses, out-houses, Edifices, Buildings, stables,
Yards, Gardens, Compounds, Wells, Tanks, Brab Trees,
Date Trees, and all other Trees, ways, water courses, paths,
commons, common of pasture and other commonable rights,
passages, privileges, and appurtenances, whatsoever to the
said villages lands hereditaments and premises hereby released or otherwise assured or intended to be or to any of

them belonging or in anywise appurtaining and the reversion and reversions remainder and remainders Rents issues and profits of the said Village Lands hereditaments and premises and every part and parcel of the same with their and every of their rights members and appurtenances and all the Estate right title Interest Term and Terms for years property possession and Equity of Redemption claim and demand whatsoever both at Law and in Equity of the said Company of in to out of or upon the said Lands or Villages or any of them or any part thereof Together with all Deeds evidences and writings now in the custody or power of the said Company relating to or concerning the same. To have and to hold the Villages Lands inhabited and waste cultivated and uncultivated hereditaments and premises mentioned to be hereby granted and released with their appurtenance unto the said Framji Cowasji his Heirs Executors administrators and assigns To the only proper use and behoof of the said Framji Cowasji his Heirs Executors administrators and assigns for ever free from all Rent arrears of Rent reserved and also from the Abkaree and all other rates taxes dues duties and assessments of what nature or kindsoever but subject Nevertheless to the restrictions in and by the said Cowls imposed and also to all such other Restrictions as the said Company shall at any time think fit to impose with respect to the sale of Liquor in the said Island of Salsette or any part thereof. And the said Company for themselves their successors and assigns do hereby covenant promise and agree to and with the said Framji Cowasji his Heirs Executors Administrators and Assigns that the said Framji Cowasji his Heirs Executors administrators and assigns shall and may at all times hereinafter have and enjoy the absolute property and right of ownership of into and over all Brab Trees Date Trees and other trees now growing standing or being or

which shall at any time or times hereinafter grow or be on
any of the Lands or Grounds hereditaments and premises
herby released or intended so to be and shall and may at
all times receive take and enjoy the rents produce and
profits thereof to his and their own use and benefit free
and absolutely discharged of and from all such rent Taxes
rates dues duties assessments and impositions as aforesaid
or otherwise howsoever and that they the said Company
their successors or assigns shall not nor will at any time or
times hereafter seize sequester or take possession of any of
the aforesaid Villages Lands hereditaments and premises
hereby granted and released or intended so to be or any
part thereof for or by reason of any rent or arrears of rent
debt or debts or other liabilities whatsoever due or demand-
able from any cultivator or cultivators residing on the said
Lands hereditaments and premises any part thereof and
further that for and notwithstanding any act Deed
matter or thing whatsoever by the said Company or
by any person or persons claiming for under or in
trust for them made done committed or suffered to
the contrary they the said Company have in themselve
good right full power and lawful and absolute authority
to grant bargain sell release and assure the said Lands
Villages and premises mentioned to be hereby granted and released and every part and parcel of the
same with their and every of their appurtenances unto
and to the use of the said Framji Cowasji his Heirs
Executors administrators and assigns in manner aforesaid
according to the true intent and meaning of these presents
(and that it shall and may be lawful to and for the said
Framji Cowasji his Heirs executors administrators and assigns peaceably and quietly to enter into and upon have hold
use occupy possess and enjoy the said Lands and Villages
hereby released or otherwise assured or intended so to be and

to receive and take the rents issues and profits thereof and of
every part thereof to and for his and their own use and benefit and without any let suit trouble eviction ejection expul-
sion hinderance interruption claim or demand whatsoever of
or by the said Company or of or by any person or persons
lawfully claiming from or under or in trust for them (and
that free and clear and freely and clearly acquitted exonerat-
ed released and for ever discharged of from and against all
other gifts grants bargains sales Leases mortgages Rents
arrears of Rents judgments executions extents suits Decrees
Debts of record debts to the King's Majesty sequestrations
Estates Titles Troubles trusts grants Bargains sales charges
or incumbrances whatsoever had made done committed
occasioned permitted or suffered by the said Company or
by any person or persons lawfully claiming or to claim
from or under in trust for them and further that the said
Company their successors and assigns and all and every other
person or persons whomsoever having or claiming or who
shall or may have or claim any estate right Title or interest
at Law or in equity into or out of the said Villages Lands
hereditaments and premises hereby released or otherwise
assured or intended so to be or any part thereof by from
through under or in trust for them shall and will from time
to time and at all times hereafter upon the reasonable
request and at the proper costs and charges nevertheless of
the said Framji Cawasji his Heirs Executors administrators and assigns make do and execute or cause and procure
to be made done and executed all such further and other
lawful and reasonable acts Deeds conveyances and assurances
in the Law whatsoever for the further better more perfectly
lawfully and absolutely or satisfactorily granting releasing
and confirming or otherwise assuring the said Lands and
Villages unto and to the use of the said Framji Cowasji

his Heirs Excutors administrators and assigns as by the
said Framji Cowasji his Heirs executors administrators
and assigns or his or their Counsel learned in the Law shall
be reasonably advised devised or required. And this
Indenture further witnesseth and the said Framji Cowasji
for himself his heirs executors and administrators doth
hereby promise covenant and agree to and with the said
Honorable Company their successors and assigns that he
the said Framji Cowasji his Heirs Executors and administrators shall and will when and so soon as he or they
or any of them shall be thereunto required by the said
Company their successors or assigns make sign seal and
deliver such Deed or other sufficient Instrument for securing
the due supply of water for the purposes and in manner
herein before in that behalf particularly mentioned as by
the said Company their Successors or assigns their Counsel
learned in the Law shall be deemed reasonable expedient in
that behalf IN WITNESS wherof the Right Honorable the
Governor in Council at Bombay aforesaid for and on behalf
of the said East India Company hath caused the common
seal of the said Company to be set and affixed to one part
thereof remaining with the said Framji Cowasji and the
said Framji Cowasji hath set his hand and seal to the
other part hereof remaining with the said Governor in
Council the day and year first above written.

Sealed and delivered   (Sd.)   E. H. Townsend,
in the presence of   Acting Secretary to Government.

(Sd.) W. Blowers.

(„) Jowdeen Narker.

At the time of Framji's coming in possession of the Poway Estate, it had at the most a population of about one hundred souls, and an income scarcely equal to the annuity laid on it. By his personal exertion and application, it was soon changed into a " LAND OF GOLD."

He first of all had a fine crop of sugarcane, from which he manufactured red sugar, he then planted and grew indigo, opium and coffee. Next he planted Mulberry and reared silk-worms, and thus by and bye transferred the waste land into a true *Celestial* city. Not only these, but he had all sorts of vegetation and fruits, even tea and Nilgiri potatoes grown there. He had innumerable Mango trees planted on his Estate, and every year gave his tenants these sweet friuts free. Framji is said to have spent upwards of five laks of rupees in improving and fertilizing his Estate. He had sunk several wells, made smooth and levelled the roads, built some fine bungalows, and a large spacious one for travellers. Scarcely any distinguished man, who happened to put his foot in Bombay, had not done him the honor to visit his Estate and speak in high terms of its fertility. It was Framji's pride to speak to his friends " I have one lak of Mango-trees planted on my Estate and supposing for a time, that each tree yields a profit of one rupee a year, I would be leaving to my family an yearly income of a lak of rupees." From this it can be seen how splendid and valuable this estate had been in the time of Framji.

Sir John Malcolm, the then Governor of Bombay, paid a visit with his staff to Framji's Poway estate on the 3rd of December 1830. He was highly delighted with the improvements made therein, as well as the Machinery for Manufacturing sugar, and as an appreciation of Mr. Framji's good work, he presented him with a gold watch and chain, he had with him at the time. On the 17th of

November 1831, the Earl of Clare, the then Governor of Bombay, together with his staff, visited Framji's Poway estate. He went all round with Framji and greatly admired the distillery for producing country-liquor, and was highly pleased to see Framji growing sugar, indigo, opium, tea, coffee, &c. also rearing silk-worms. His Excellency observed that it was a wonder that in the short space of only a couple of years, Framji had brought about so extensive an improvement. After taking lunch with Framji, His Excellency presented him with a shawl valued at Rs. 1,400 in appreciation of his good services. Framji in a few appropriate words thanked His Excellency for his kindness. After remaining the whole day as the guest of Framji, His Excellency returned highly pleased.

Framji had received several prizes from the "Agri Horticultural Society" amongst which may be noticed :—

A prize of Rs. 30 for growing Nilgiri Potatoes on the 24th of February 1831.

A prize of Rs. 130 for rearing silk-worms and producing silk therefrom and also for growing rice, opium, &c., on the 13th of May 1831.

A prize of Rs. 50 for producing the best loaf-sugar on the 24th January 1832.

A prize of Rs. 30 for growing the best Mangoes on the 27th May 1832.

A prize of Rs. 50 for growing coffee, Chinese Lime, Oranges, Apples and other fruits on the 6th of January 1835.

A prize of Rs. 35 for producing silk-worms reared on his soil on the 5th of May 1835.

Framji Cowasji was the first Parsee, nay the first Native of India, who on the 18th of May 1838 ventured to send a present of that sweet and delicious fruit the Bombay mangoes to Her Most Gracious Majesty the Queen-Empress.

The following is the document, which accompanied the offering :—

To Her Most Gracious Majesty the
QUEEN of ENGLAND.

May it please your Majesty,

The improvement and extension of steam navigation have now happily brought your Majesty's dominions at home and your dominions in the Eastern world so closely together, that I venture most humbly and most respectfully to lay at your Majesty's feet some specimens of the celebrated Bombay Mangoes, in the earnest hope that this delicious fruit, which has never been transmitted to Europe may reach your Majesty in a state of preservation and prove acceptable. Such precautions have been adopted to preserve the fruit as appear most efficacious, but if the botanists of your Majesty's dominions at home can prescribe a preferable method, it shall be adopted in the transmission of further supplies of this or any other kind of fruit peculiar to the country which has not hitherto been seen in Great Britain.

Your Majesty's most obedient and faithful,
Eastern Subject,

Bombay, 18th May 1838. (Sd.) FRAMJI COWASJI.

" In acknowledgment of this present, the master of the household conveyed to him the Queen's approbation of the zeal and enterprise evinced by him, and Her Majesty's gratification at the dutiful expression of loyalty by which it was accompanied."

Indeed, splendid was the Poway Estate, and would no doubt have continued the same, if proper care and attention were paid to it, but alas ! for the discord and disunion going on among the several of the leading descendants of this ever respected and noble gentleman, the estate has been in litigation for upwards of twenty years, and Poway is now but a shadow of its past greatness and splendour.

CHAPTER VII.

Framji's minor charities.

Framji's charity was universal, he held no distinction of caste or creed, wherever he saw a necessity he was ever ready to render a helping hand. His benevolence was not merely limited to the Fraternity of which he was a member, nor did it terminate in his own country. Besides the several great works of Public utility narrated in the foregone pages, he at times did many more smaller acts of charity. He was ever foremost in all matters concerning public interest.

Framji gave the first Kadmi Gumbar feast on the 22nd of October 1805.

In the year 1811, Framji along with others contributed to a "service plate" worth Rs. 15,750, presented to Sir Charles Forbes on his retiring after twenty-two years of public life in Bombay.

Framji subscribed Rs. 1,250 towards the relief of the famine-stricken people of the North on the 10th December 1812.

On the 24th of May 1814, Framji with several other leading Native gentlemen protested against the Police *Zulum* in carrying away stray dogs, cows and such other domestic animals.

In the year 1814, Framji was elected a Director of the "Bombay Insurance Society."

On the 9th of September 1815, Framji gave the sum of Rs. 200 towards the fund for building the "Calidonian Asylum" for the orphans of the Scottish Army and Navy.

Framji contributed in 1816, Rs. 200 towards the fund for supporting the family of those soldiers who fought under the Duke of Wellington at the battle of Waterloo.

On the 8th of June 1816, Framji was nominated along with three others to a Committee to appeal to the Imperial Government against the wrong done by the Bombay Government.

In the year 1823 Framji contributed to a memorial and " Plate " worth 400 Guineas presented to the Hon'ble Mr. Alexander Bell on his departure from Bombay.

On the 10th August 1820, Framji was elected a Member of the " Native School and School Book Committee."

In the year 1824, Framji subscribed to a " Piece of Plate " worth 700 Guineas presented to me, James Henry Crawford, a retiring Merchant and Magistrate of Bombay.

On the 15th of April 1825, Framji subscribed to a " Piece of Plate " worth £500 presented to Lieutenant Colonel William Brooks, Civil Architect, who retired after forty-two years' service in Bombay.

On the 21st of September 1825, Framji subscribed Rs. 300 towards the " Native Education Society's Building Fund."

Framji contributed £5 15s. towards the " Royal National Institute " on the 21st January 1826. He was one of the two contributors to the fund, Sir Jamsetji Jeejibhoy being the other.

On the 16th of August 1827, Framji gave Rs. 100 towards the relief of the sick and strange sailors in England.

Framji on the 28th August 1828, subscribed Rs. 7,000 for perpetuating the memory of the Right Hon'ble Mountsteuart Elphinstone, the then retiring Governor of Bombay.

On the 30th of May 1828, Framji gave Rs. 100 towards the improvement of " East Indians."

Framji was elected the Vice-President of the Indian Agricultural and Horticultural Society on the 4th February 1830.

Framji subscribed to a " Piece of Plate " valued at 300 Guineas presented to Dr. William Jafferson on the 5th of June 1830, on his retiring from the Ophthalmic Institution in Bombay.

On the 15th November 1830, Framji let out a floor of his house at Meadow Street, for the use of the " Bombay General Library " on a nominal rent of Rs. 75 a month.

Framji subscribed Rs. 100 towards the furnishing of the " Bombay Theatre House " on the 27th November 1830.

On the 14th of January 1832, Framji subscribed to a " Piece of Plate " valued at £1,500 presented to the Hon'ble John Romer, the retiring member of Council.

On the 3rd January 1831 Framji built the Tower of Silence at a cost of Rs. 20,000 in memory of his deceased daughter Bai Dinbai.

Framji on the 3rd May 1832, gave Rs. 1,000 to the Parsee Panchayat for reparing the surrounding of the " Towers of Silence " and Rs. 1,000 to the Fire Temple at Persia.

Framji gave a sum of Rs. 200 towards the " Famine Relief Fund " in the Southern Districts on the 25th July 1833.

On the 28th June 1834, Framji was appointed to the Committee for suggesting the improvements in roads.

On the 30th of October 1834, Framji with some other leading natives came forward to establish the " Panjrapole " in Bombay.

Framji gave Rs. 500 at the *Oothamna* ceremony of his father on the 18th December 1835 in several Panchayat charity funds.

On the 28th of February 1835 Framji subscribed Rs. 1,000 to the establishment of the " Earl of Clare Scholarship " in connection with the Elphinstone College.

On the 3rd of October 1835, Framji was chosen a Member on the board of " Bombay Native Dispensary."

On the 2nd of May 1836, Framji subscribed Rs. 1,000 towards the brodening of the City Gates of Bombay at Church Gate and Bazaar Gate.

On the 24th September 1836, Framji was elected a Member of the " Bombay Chamber of Commerce."

Framji contributed Rs. 200 towards the Captain Chand's Testimonial Fund on the 27th December 1886.

On the 1st of January 1837, Framji was elected a non-resident member of the Royal Asiatic Society of Great Britain and Ireland.

Framji, on the 22nd April 1837, subscribed Rs. 200 towards Captain James Hersbery's memorial.

On the 3rd May 1837, Framji gave Rs. 3,000 towards the " Surat Fire Relief Fund."

Framji contributed Rs. 200 on the 6th of Janury 1838, towards putting up a new clock in St. Thomas' Cathedral in the Fort.

On the 29th March 1838, Framji subscribed Rs. 1,000 towards the North-West Provinces Famine Relief Fund.

Framji subscribed Rs. 1,000 to the Sir Robert Grant's Memorial Fund on the 28th of July 1838.

Framji gave Rs. 1,500 at the *Oothamna* ceremony of his friend Framji Dossabhoy Jamshedji Wadia, on the 13th of August 1838, towards the building of a new Tower of Silence.

In January 1839, Framji subscribed Rs. 1,000 to the "Bombay District Benevolent Society," and was elected a Life Governor and a Vice-President of the Society.

It is said that the big tank known as the "*Dhobi Talao*" situated near Marine Quarters, opposite the Money School, was dug during the time of the Portugese Government, by a washerman for the use of his fellow countrymen, and was hence known after him as *Dhobi Talao.*Owing to the filthy use of the people, the waters had become quite dirty, and owing to a scarcity of water in the year 1839 this tank had almost dried up. On the 18th of April 1839, Framji undertook to have it cleansed and deepened at his own expense. At a cost of nearly Rs. 40,000, Framji had the tank thoroughly rebuilt on a larger scale and handed it over to the Government for the public use. In recognition of this noble act the well was henceforth known as "The Framji Cowasji Tank." On the 8th of January 1840 Sir J. R. Carnack, the then Governor of Bombay, paid a visit to this newly built tank and also Framji's Mugbhat Oart, and was highly pleased with the arrangement for water supply made by Framji. He in few appropriate words eulogised Mr. Framji's work and presented him with a shawl. The following is the tablet attached on the tank :—

FRAMJI COWASJI TANK.

That tank was so called by order of Government, to commemorate the late Framji Cowasji's liberality, in expending a large sum of money, on its reconstruction, in the year 1839.

On the 16th September 1839, Framji contributed Rs. 300 towards the building of a Fire-Temple at Calcutta by his brother Rustomji.

Framji was one of the bold and warm projectors among the natives in the establishment of the " Bank of Bombay," in which he then subscribed 159 shares, to the extent of a lac and fifty thousand rupees, and which establishment has since then become productive of so many salutory results to the mercantile community of this island. It was opened in the year 1840 and Framji was elected a Director.

On the 6th of April 1840, Framji subscribed Rs. 1,000 towards the erecting of Sir Charles Forbes' Statue.

In 1841 Framji was nominated an " Honorary Commissioner of the Court of Requests."

On the 22nd April 1841, Framji subscribed Rs. 1,000 to Sir J. R. Carnack's Memorial.

Framji gave a sum of Rs 500 to Sir J. J. Translation Fund on the 5th of June 1842.

On the 13th of June 1842, Framji contributed Rs. 300 towards presenting a " Piece of Plate " to Mr. James Mathewson.

In July 1842, Framji entertained Sir Jamsetji Jeejibhoy, Bart., to a party in honour of his gaining the Knighthood.

In 1843 Framji was appointed a Director of the " Bank of Western India."

Framji on the 4th of June 1844 gave Rs. 100 towards the Elphinstone Institution Endowment Fund.

Framji contributed Rs. 300 towards presenting a " Piece of Plate " to the Hon'ble Mr. J. W. Anderson on the 10th February 1844.

On the 28th of March 1844, Framji contributed Rs. 150 towards presenting a " Piece of Plate " to Dr. William Macrie."

Framji gave the sum of Rs. 101 to be distributed amongst the officers of the Garrison and Navy, who assisted in putting out the great fire in the Fort on the 2nd of April 1844.

On the 24th of August 1844, Framji contributed Rs. 100 towards presenting a " Piece of Plate " to Major General Sir Henry Pottinger, Bart.

On the 17th September 1844, Framji built the Fire-Temple at Churney Road.

Framji gave the sum of Rs. 1,500 towards the building of the Lady Jamsetjee Road at Mahim on the 8th April 1845.

On the 15th of April 1845, Framji contributed the sum of Rs. 5,000 towards the rebuilding of the " Banaji Agiari."

Framji subscribed Rs. 2,000 to the " Gumbhar Funds," in memory of his deceased daughter Maneckbai, on the 8th of June 1845.

Framji headed the list of a protest sent the Court of Directors against the increase in opium duty from Rs. 125 to Rs. 200 in the year 1845.

On the 30th of October 1845, Framji gave the sum of Rs. 300 towards the " Patan Panjrapole."

Framji contributed Rs. 1,150 towards the Ireland Famine Fund, on the 4th of June 1846.

In 1848 Framji founded a prize for regularity in the " Grant Medical College," and also subscribed Rs. 100 to the Students' Literary and Scientific Society's Funds.

Framji contributed Rs. 100 to the Reed Scholarship.

In 1850 Framji gave the sum of Rs. 100 for establishing a Lying-in Hospital.

CHAPTER VIII.

Building of the " Tower of Silence " and the
" Fire Temple."

The Fire Temple raised by Framji Cowasji and his brothers, to facilitate the worship of God after the manner of their fathers, and the Tower of Silence constructed for the reception of the body after death, at a cost of over four lacs of rupees, are permanent memorials of his piety and his respect for the usages of his ancient religion.

On the 6th of May 1831 Framji lost his daughter Dinbai, and to perpetuate the memory of his beloved daughter, Framji thought of erecting a Tower of Silence. He set aside a sum of Rs. 20,000 for the purpose and promised to pay more, if requred. For this, Framji wrote to Bai Buchubai, the widow of the late Ardeshir Dadysett, asking her to give him a plot of land on the Chowpati Hill, for the building of the Tower of Silence, which was readily granted. On the 3rd of June of the same year the ceremony of laying the foundation-stone of the Tower of Silence was performed, where more than twelve thousand Parsees had gathered together from different parts of the country, to witness the ceremony. On the 3rd of May 1832 the building was completed and it was consecrated by Dustoor Rustomji Kaikobadji Mullafeeroz, before a large gathering of Parsees brought from far and distant villages. Framji had, by advertising in the local papers, invited his castemen from all quarters ; not only that, but had through his influence got all the Parsees, either in Government service or private firms, a holiday. Framji had several tents pitched all over the Panchayat ground for his guests from up-country, and entertained them all during their stay in Bombay. The Tower of Silence was designed and built under the superintendence of Mr. Sorabji Dhunjibhoy Poonagur, one of the first batch of Parsee engineers in Bombay. On the 13th of April 1832, the Rt. Hon'ble the

Earl of Clare, the then Governor of Bombay, visited the
" Banaji Tower of Silence," and on the 17th of December
1833, a wooden model of this Tower was sent through the
Hon'ble Sir William Newnham to be put at the " Royal
Asiatic Society of Great Britain and Ireland."

As a grateful son, Framji thought of perpetuating the
names of his respected parents—Cowasji and Bai Jaiji—in
connection with some sacred building. With this view he,
in part with his brothers, Messrs. Curshedji and Rustomji
and his nephew Mr. Dadabhoy Rustomji, erected the great
" Fire Temple" known as the *Banaji Atash Behram*" situated
at Churney Road, opposite the Railway station. It was in-
augurated in great pomp before a large gathering on the
13th of December 1845 by Dustur Jamsetji Edalji Jam-
aspasana, assisted by Dustur Bezonji Rustomji, who was
afterwards put in the charge of it. The inauguration ceremony was a grand and interesting one. The total cost of
this building is said to have gone to about two lacs and a
half, of which Framji alone subscribed a lac, and moreover
set aside the two villages—Kanjur and Vikhrote—yielding
an income of Rs. 2,500 per annum for its daily maintenance.
He further set apart a large sum of money for holding
Gumbhars (caste-feasts) and Jasans, which fund now amounts
to about Rs. 75,000. On the 12th of July 1842 Framji had
a " Deed-pole " executed by Mr. William Auckland, the
then Advocate-General, by which he appointed his two
sons Pestonji and Nanabhoy Framji, and his nephew Dadabhoy Rustomji Banaji, as Managers, and Messrs. Rustomji
Cowasji Banaji, Maneckji Rustomji Banaji, and Dhunjibhoy
Behramji Rana, as trustees of the same.

On the 4th of November 1858, at the *Oothamna* ceremony
of Bai Buchubai, the widow of late Framji Cowasji, her
grandsons Messrs. Navrosji Nanabhoy Framji, Sorabji Pestonji Framji, Behramji Nanabhoy Framji, and Hormusji
Pestonji Framji, subscribed amongst themselves a fund
of about Rs. 5,000, for building a house in the compound of
the Fire Temple, for the residence of the Dustoor in charge.

CHAPTER IX.

His connection with Public Adventures.

Framji was one of the bold adventurers among the natives in embarking his capital with the few Europeans in the establishment of the "Great Eastern Peninsula Railway," which was the first start of its kind in Bombay. He had in the year 1844, taken up 200 shares of the Company to the extent of a lac of rupees ; but much to the discredit of other subscribers, who kept altogether backwards at the moment of difficulty experienced in cutting the line through the Ghats, which eventually led to the breaking up of the Company, he warmly espoused this object and worked with energy and assiduity with Mr. Clarke, the then Railway Engineer. Notwithstanding his exertions, the scheme fell to the ground, till at last it was taken up in England by the "Great Indian Peninsula Railway Company," who are now greatly extending the line to the great advantage of national utility and importance. The following is a letter from Mr. T. Williamson, speaking highly of Mr. Framji's public spirit :—

My DEAR FRAMJI,   LONDON, *3rd June* 1845.

At my suggestion a Prospectus of the "Great Indian Railway" has been sent you. I am in hopes this Company will form a junction with Mr. Clarke and give its views, strength and support. I admired your public spirit in following Mr. Clarke's undertaking, disregarding the apprehensions and prejudices, which, I understand, have hampered that gentleman, and thrown obstacles in the way of a great work calculated to be of such benefit to the agricultural and commercial interests of India generally, and Bombay particularly. I would give a good deal to pass through "Poway" and again witness your improvements. Believe me, with kind regards to you,

My Dear Framji,

Yours very sincerely,

(Sd.) THOMAS WILLIAMSON.

His ever active mind and penetrating genius was not at rest even here, it soon paved the way for another bold and daring enterprise of the above kind the "Cotton Spinning and Weaving Company," in which he had taken up 100 shares of the aggregate value of Rs. 50,000. But it also soon met the sad fate of its sister scheme, on account of the lukewarm interest of the several subscribers to it. It came into existence and died soon after, but did not live long enough to thrive and bear the sweet fruits it promised.

It is generally the case, that great and novel undertakings have always been hindered in the first start with obstacles very serious, which, if not judiciously overcome in the very beginning, take a firmer root, and put the whole scheme, however beneficial it may be, to the ground. Such was the sad fate with which both these schemes of the greatest importance and benefit to the interests of Bombay met, and at last fell to the ground. Another thing, greatly to be deplored in the native society here, is that they have not the enterprising spirit to take to a great and hazardous undertaking. They are wanting in the spirit and energy to continue the same zeal and anxiety with which they started it, and thus many a great undertaking has been allowed to be entombed in its very cradle. Under these circumstances individual exertions are of little avail and, as must naturally be the case, the scale of balance always turns to the greater side, and popular side gains the triumph, whether true or false. The case with India is as yet different from that of other countries in Europe; it cannot yet be put on a standard of equality with them; the populace of India is not a thinking one, it does not think for itself; it is led by some single individuals. These leaders must be such as could judiciously guard against the sudden changes of popular opinion. India has but yet produced few leaders of this type. In Framji, Bombay at least found such a leader as we speak of. His active mind was not at rest, till it had achieved some mighty object of the greatest national utility and importance. He failed in some, but we can, under no circumstances allude these failures to his want of energy, tact, or perseverance. We said it once, and we say it again, that it will take a long long time for the populace of India to be a thinking body.

He exerted his spirits to the utmost but was grieved to see national works of the gravest importance fall to the ground on account of the cold-heartedness of a large multitude of his countrymen, but what could individual exertions do before so large a multitude, whose minds were biased by the slightest suspicion in a great and enterprising undertaking.

In Framji were nurtured the embryo thought of a " Polytechnic Institute " and the " School of Industry." He had at heart the establishment óf an Institute of the sort now started amongst us. Many a time and oft he expressed his opinion to establish an Institution, where the different branches of artistic professions may be taught on the improved plan of similar Institutions in Europe, and this was really a sad want amongst us. This will at once convey to the minds of our readers, the strength of a naturally fertile genius, though uncultivated by the sublimities of a refined education and a ripe and profound science.

Framji was equally fond of pleasure as he was of mercantile enterprise. In the year 1842, he introduced gas-light in his residence at Mazagon, which was then looked with surprise and astonishment. Crowds of people of all caste and creed thronged at his place to have a sight of this " novel light."

Framji was himself fond of studying English and Vernacular works, and he cultivated this taste to a great extent, not only in himself, but as already noted, in his family also. Though not a great scholar, he could write and speak English very correctly.

Framji was at the same time a staunch Zorastrian, and did every thing in his power to promote his religion. With a view to spread the knowledge of Zorastrianism among his community, he had, at great expense, several Zand, Persian and Phelvi works of great authors translated into Gujrati. The first of these works, which he gave to the reading public, was the Gujrati translation of " *Tajkartel Hookma*," a Persian philosophical work, translated by Mr. Dossabhoy Sorabji Munshee in the year 1818. Framji further gave a sum of Rs. 5,000 for the translation of several religious works, such as " The Vandidad " and the " Yajasnee."

CHAPTER X.

His Disposition, the last days of his life,
His Wife and Children.

Though haughty in appearance, Framji was very kind
and always forgiving. He was so great an enthusiast of
truth and independence, that he not for a moment hesitated
to point out the defects and wrong doings of his best friends,
nearest relatives, and even those of the richest men. He
ever adhered to the truth, and under no circumstances, however trying, severed an inch from the path of honesty. He
had always a great aversion to mean flatterers or sycophants,
but was ever ready to render a helping hand to even the
meanest of his countrymen, when he saw that he was really
in need. He held the rich and the poor alike. Simple
in his diet, he thought it one of the accomplishments to go
about in as simple a dress as possible.

Though not born in affluent circumstances, by shere
perseverance, honesty and diligence, he rose to be one of
the greatest and respected merchants of the day. Not only
was his fame confined to his own community in Bombay,
but it had spread itself among all classes of Europeans and
natives in even far and remote countries. In latter part of
his career, he fell a victim to the vicissitudes of time ; he
bore it with patience, and even then, did not shrink for a
time from those noble qualities. The latter part of his
life was rather a troubled one, both from pecuniary loss,
and domestic quarrels. He was not pleased with the conduct of his sons, especially that of the eldest one.

A very interesting and at the same time remarkable
instance, of the way in which Framji administered justice
in his capacity, as the leading member of the Parsee Panchayat, is related as follows. On one occasion, a Parsee

applied to the Panchayat for separation from his wife. The other Settias, referred him to Framji, being questioned by that gentleman the grounds on which he claimed separation from his wife, the Parsee after some hesitation said that she was black and he did not like her. Framji after some consideration, asked that Parsee to call on a certain day at his place. As previously arranged, Framji called the wife of that Parsee and her parents to his place that day, prior to that man's coming. Framji had them sitted in a room and took his seat by the side of his wife in the front hall. The other members of the Punchayat were also invited on that occasion, and made to sit in another room, Framji then sent for the Parsee and made him sit near him, and once more asked him on what grounds he claimed separation from his wife, after some hesitation, he repeated that she was black and he did not like her. Pointing to his own wife, who was sitting next to him, Framji said " I hope your wife is not blacker than the lady sitting here. Do you know who she is ? She is my wife. It is through her that I command so much influence and respect. Perhaps it might be in your lot some better prospects through her. Go, take her with you and respect and love her as your true wife." The Parsee was greatly ashamed of his folly and is said to have shed tears. Framji then summoned his other colleagues and the wife of that man and her parents together and joined the couple hand in hand, and after treating them to dinner, made the couple presents of wedding clothes and sent them home. This will show what a good and magnanimous heart Framji had.

Framji was labouring for some time under an incurable urine disease, and was under the treatment of the best medical men, who paid him every attention and care. Their efforts, at last, proved unsuccessful, and he departed this life on the 12th February 1851, at the matured age of eighty-five, at his residence at Mazagon. He was greatly dissatisfied with the misconduct of his sons, and in the last Will which he was preparing some time prior to his death, he intended to set aside all his sons and nominate two of his grandsons, Messrs. Naorosji Nanabhoy Framji, and Sorabji Pestonji Framji, as his heirs and executors, along with his widow, but unfortunately this Will remained unexecuted at the last moment. Though his death was an expected one, it came all of a sudden. A little before his demise, he rose with all intention to sign this new Will, in the presence of his solicitor and doctor, but to the great surprise and sudness of all those present, while coming from the water closet, he fell never to rise again. Under these circumstances the new Will remained unexecuted, and an old Will of a remote date, so far back as the year 1828 A.D., was resorted to. By this Will his widow became the sole executrix, the court appointing Mr. Cursetji Nusservanji Cama, a respectable merchant of Bombay, her legal attorney to wind up the affairs of the deceased.

The s s. Suliman was wrecked on the coast of Madras on the 24th of May 1850, and the s.s. Buckingham was distroyed by fire at Calcutta in the year 1851. These two serious losses told heavily on Framji.

Framji left a large amount of debt behind him, but so extensive was his estate, that after his death all his creditors were paid in full with interest. Thus ended the brilliant and splendid career of a truely great and glorious man, kind and bestowing in his nature, one in whom there was a store of genius and activity, one who was familiar with all the topics of the day, one who was resorted to for justice, one in whom were centered uprightness, faithfulness and fidelity, one who adorned each and every assembly, and one who was the head of his community.

Like her husband, Bai Buchubai, the wife of Framji, was kind-hearted and benevolent. She considered her happiness in the welfare of her husband and in relieving the distress of the aggrieved. To her arbitration many intricate cases of family disunion and discord were resorted to and both the parties returned satisfied with her decision. She was a very religious lady and till the last moment of her death she observed strict piety. She had given away large sums of money to poor relatives. On the 2nd of November 1858 she breathed her last at the good old age of 92. It was her last solace and consolation to learn from her constituted attorney, that all the creditors of her late husband were paid in full, and she was only satisfied as to the truth of this statement, when all the creditors were called before her to varify it. Framji had four sons, namely, Jehangir, Edalji, Nanabhoy and Pestonji, and five daughters, namely, Rutonbai, the wife of Nusservanji Rustomji Rana, Navajbai, the wife of Dhanjibhoy Byramji Rana, Meherbai, the wife of Pestonji Navrosji Banaji, Maneckbai, the wife of Dadabhoy Rustomji Banaji, and Peerojbai, the wife of Ardeshir Curshedji Dadysett.

CHAPTER XI.

His Obituary Notice.

The *Bombay Times* of 13th February 1851 says :—

It is with much regret that we have to intimate the demise of one of the most venerable and respected members of our native community, Framji Cowasji Banaji, Esq., of Bandhoop (Poway), who died at his residence, Mazagon, yesterday morning, in the 82nd year of his age. Framji Cowasji commenced business as a merchant about the year 1790 ; in 1795 we find him agent for the Hon'ble the East India Company, and down to within a few months of the present time he has, for considerably upwards of half a century, been one of the most able and upright of our merchants, and one of the most zealous and indefatigable promoters of moral and physical improvement. He was one of the most active of those who shared or assisted in the great educational movement, at its height in the bright and memorable era of our history, Mr. Elphinstone's time— to which so many auspicious events are referred, and on which the memory so delights to dwell. He was a member of the Education Board from the time of its establishment till advancing years and increasing infirmities induced him a few months since to withdraw, when he found himself unable longer to discharge the duties in the manner he desired. His notions of native education were from the outset in strict accordance with the views so often expressed in these columns, and nearly a quarter of a century ago, he recommended a system of instruction similar to that only now beginning to make its appearance amongst us,—that which enables the pupil in after life to earn his bread, or add to his resources or comforts. He, some sixteen years ago, proposed to Lord Clare, a branch establishment to our other seminaries, precisely similar to that embraced in the plan of our Polytechnic Institute, where carpenters, blacksmiths, glaziers and other artificers should be taught to perform the tasks assigned to them, better, or with a less expenditure, of time or labour, than heretofore ; and here those classes of the community, who must look to the labour of their hands the means of their support, should learn how to do so with most advantage and effect. The luxury of literature, or accomplishments of abstract science, he reserved for those who had time, leisure and wealth enough for their attainment or enjoyment. Common sense views such as these, long scouted in practice, have since been fully recognised by Sir Erskine Perry and Mr. Willougby, as they have not only been recognised, but acted on, with infinite advantage by Colonel Jervis—the three distinguished men, we have named respectively representing the three great sections of the educationists amongst us. Framji Cowasji was one of the greatest of our agricultural improvers, and the efforts he made on his estate of Poway in Salsette, and its neighbourhood, long justly entitled him to the name of the Lord Leicester of Western India. A vast addition to the number of the European community, and increase to the mercantile enterprise of the presidency, having been occasioned by the operations of the New Charter, fostered as they were by the exertions of a succession of able and patriotic administrations in the period just preceding 1840, it became apparent that new life blood was wanted in the press, and that newspapers must from henceforth have much more important tasks to perform than the announcement of the reliefs of the Army, the chronicling of the movements of the Governor, or festivals at Government House, the accidents of the chase, or calamities of famine or conflagration. A free press was desiderated for the advocacy of public measures, now that freedom of discussion had been permitted to newspapers, and a public created for their perusal, while the opening up of the overland communication was beginning to permit the transmission of enlightenment to the people at home through the journals of India. To this, as to all other changes in the political sky, the subject of our notice was fully alive, and Framji Cowasji was one of the first of those who exerted himself to bring into existence the journal which now chronicles his demise. He lived to receive back again seven times told the amount of his original investments from an adventure entered on without view to profit. With a feeling of fraternal duty which does them honor, Framji and Curshedji Cowasji had become securities for their brother Rustomji Cowasji, a distinguished Calcutta merchant, chiefly engaged in the China trade, whose goodness of heart and integrity are celebrated by all who know him. Four years since Rustomji overtaken by one of those commercial reverses which often prove fatal to the most circumspect and honorable, became unable to meet the claims against him ; and his brothers in their efforts to assist him became involved to an extent they had never dreamt of. Curshedji Cowasji died three years since ; Framji is now cut off in a ripe old age, but though not in poverty, with a fortune vastly reduced from what he had possessed through the greater part of his life. The intelligence, kind-heartedness, and benevolence, which formed such distinguished traits in his character, honorable as they were eclipsed by the stern integrity, the candour, truth, and perfect frankness, for which through life he was conspicuous. Though old age had of late years made him garrulous, it had diminished none of the qualities by which he had all along been marked ; and the same clear views of things ; the same sound sense and far seeing sagacity for which through life he had been remarkable, continued to mainfest themselves to the last.

78

CHAPTER XII.

Some of the correspondences between Mr. Framji Cowasji and the Government about Abkaree.

No. 1113 of 1838.

To

FRAMJI COWASJI, Esquire,

&c.,　　&c.,　　&c.,

Bombay.

Sir,

You have, I believe, been for some time past in the knowledge that the Hon'ble the Court of Directors are desirous of entering into an arrangement with you respecting a repurchase of the rights of Abkaree conveyed to you by Government in a deed of Sale of your Poway Estate. My Assistant Mr. Davies has likewise stated to you the wishes of the Government that such an arrangement should be effected as soon as it conveniently could be ; may I now request the favour of your expressing your views upon this subject, having had a considerable time to take the same into your consideration.

I have the honour to be,

Sir,

Your most obedient Servant,

(Signed)　GEO. COLES,

Acting 1st Asst. Collr. in Charge.

Tanna Collector's Office,
5th September 1838.

No. 279/47.

To

THE HON'BLE GEORGE RUSSEL CLERK,

Governor and President in Council,

&c., &c., &c.,

Bombay.

HON'BLE SIR,

As the Government are desirous that I should reconvey to Government the *Abkaree* and rights therewith connected which were made over to me with the Freehold of the Poway Estate on Salsette, I beg to submit the following for your indulgent consideration.

2nd. The Poway Estate comprising several villages was granted to the late Dr. Scott, by the Bombay Government about 50 years ago, on a perpetual lease, subject to the payment of an annual rent to Government.

3rd. Dr. Scott having failed in the payment of his rent the Estate was resumed by Government, and made over to me in 1829/30, together with the *Abkaree* on a Lease in perpetuity, and the annual rental then fixed by Government being the average of the Revenue which had been realized during the ten previous years.

4th. From charitable motives I was led many years ago (in 1823) to sink wells in my Oart called Moogbhat in Bombay, for the better and constant supply of fresh water through an aqueduct to the two Reservoirs situated on the Duncan Road, for the use of the inhabitants of Camatee-poora, and the neighbouring densely populated districts ; where owing to no drinking water being procurable from wells, owing to the brackish nature of the soil, much distress prevailed from the extreme scarcity of that necessary of life.

5th. Three wells were sunk by me for this purpose and a Steam Engine set up to work a Pump, besides six Motts with six pairs of Bullocks worked to raise the water. The original outlay was Rs. 30,000 and the expenditure for establishment maintained by me up to the present time about Rs. 200 a month or Rs. 2,400 per annum.

6th. Anxious to secure the continuance of these works in perpetuity, I submitted to Government in a letter dated October 1831, the immense expenditure incurred by me in improvements on the Poway Estate, I solicited that I should be allowed to redeem the rental at 10 years purchase, proposing at the same time to appoint Government Trustees of the Estate so as to empower them to have the wells and establishment in the Oart Moogbhat kept up out of the revenues of the estate for ever. The proposition was received by the Government and the Hon'ble the Court of Directors in a liberal spirit and in the year 1837 the arrangement was completed by the Estate being made over to me in Freehold (on payment of the Government Revenue for 10 years) and a Trust Deed being executed by me to Government of the effect above stated. Thus a charitable object, involving an annual expense of Rs. 2,400 out of my estate has been perpetuated.

7th. Under the arrangement in question all that had been leased to me at an annual rental was (being redeemed by me at 10 years purchase) conveyed to me by Government in Freehold for ever, that is to say the *Abkaree* as well as the said revenue of the Estate.

8th. It appears however that the Hon'ble Court of Directors afterwards requested the Government to try and get me to give up the Abkaree revenue, and on the Collector of Tannah asking me in the year 1838 on what terms I would do so, I explained to him how great a sufferer I should be if deprived of the Abkaree, the only source from which I could expect to obtain hereafter anything like a return for the immense sums expended by me on the Estate and I expressed a hope that the grant in freehold of villages to the amount of Rupees Fifty Thousand per annum, would not under the circumstances be deemed more than an equivalent for the Abkaree to which I chiefly looked to be eventually compensated in some degree for my heavy outlays—some time afterwards I learnt from the Collector that the Hon'ble Court would not agree to these terms, the Abkaree of the Estate consequently continues with me.

9th. If the Hon'ble Court still wish me to resign the Abkaree, I beg to say that I shall not object to do so on such terms as may be considered fair and reasonable, but at the same time I would solicit favorable consideration on the following statement.

10th. In my letter of October 1831 above referred to (which was acknowledged by Government on the 16th November following) my expenditure in improving the Estate was detailed, amounting to Rupees One Lac, and forty five thousand, since then I have laid in other works of the same nature a further sum of Rupees One Lac, besides Rupees Sixty Thousand in the construction of Salt Pans in the village Kanjoor, making a total of about Rupees Three Lacs exclusive of Rupees 45,842-1-80 paid for the redemption of the rental of the Estate.

11th. The interest on the above amount at the commercial rate greatly exceeds, what is at present (or even has been) realized by me annually from the Estate, the estate has therefore been to me a source of loss instead of gain. Such a result will scarcely appear surprising to any one acquainted with the peculiarities of the soil and climate of Salsette, of which, (before I took the Estate) I had but an imperfect notion. Numerous were the endeavours made by me to raise more valuable produce than grain, and exportable articles such as Sugar, Indigo, as also to manufacture Silk, &c., they promised fairly for a time but they all proved failures in the end. Again large numbers of people were brought from other parts at different times, at great cost to me, to settle on the Estate in order to carry on the new works, but owing to the unhealthiness of Salsette to strangers especially from September to the close of the year, most of them sickened, a large portion died, and the rest abandoned the place.

12th. Although I have thus been a great loser, Government has derived no small advantage from my outlays. In one of the villages of the estate namely Kanjoor, near Bhandoop, I have constructed salt works (commenced in 1839 and about 3 Miles all round) which cost me much trouble and anxiety as well as money. There is room for 5,000 evaporating Pans, of these 2,200 are finished at a cost of Rs. 60,000, and the remainder will be made as quickly as possible as soon as more cultivators are to be got, the further expenditure required on these accounts being estimated at Rs. 80,000. These salt works were first brought into operation in 1842/43 when they produced 6531 Maunds of Salt and yielded a revenue to Government of Rs. 3,265-8-0. In 1843/44 the produce was 18765 Indian Maunds and the revenue thereon Rs. 9,382-12-0. In 1844/45 the produce was 22401 Indian Maunds, the revenue thereon Rs. 16,800. In 1845/46 the produce was 20168 Indian Maunds for which Government obtained in excise duty Rs. 15,126. In the year 1846/47 the produce was 42640 Indian Maunds on which the excise duty realized by Government amounted to Rs. 31,980-0-0. As the number of evaporating beds will be increased each year and as the produce of each bed already made will go on increasing each year as it becomes saturated with saline particles and hardened, the quantity of Salt manufactured at these works will in a few years be such as to add to the excise revenue of Government at least Seventy-five Thousand Rupees per annum or more.

13th. When the Salt works at Kanjoor are completed I propose, if circumstances should allow, to construct similar works at another village of my estate called Vickrolee near Hurreealy. One of the greatest difficulties I experienced however is the want of labourers and this want would be supplied if my estate comprized a few more villages.

14th. I need scarcely observe that while the advantage to Government is very great from the outlay of capital by me on such works, the benefits to the Ryots is also considerable besides what they earn as labourers while the works are going on many afterwards find profitable employment as manufacturers of salt while they have no occupation durign the dry season in their fields.

15th. Notwithstanding the disappointment I have experienced in respect to the profit which I expected from laying out so much money as has been expended by me on the Estate, I still hoped for some return eventually but these prospects are destroyed by the adoption of a line for the new road, so distant from Poway as to deprive the estate of the advantages it has hitherto enjoyed from the old road from Tannah to Bombay passing through it. On this subject I made a representation to Government but yielded to the wish your Honor was pleased to express that I should withdraw my objections.

16th. If the considerations above submitted should induce Government to make over to me villages yielding

such an annual sum as would compensate me for the loss
of the Abkaree of my Estate (and considering my future
prospects from the Abkaree I cannot value it at less than
Rupees Twenty-five Thousand per annum) or compensate me
for such loss by making over to me villages on Salsette to
that amount, or part of that amount, and in the latter
case, authorizing the payment to me of the remaining sum
from the General Treasury—I shall be glad to resign the
Abkaree to Government as it has ever been a rule with
me to pay the greatest attention in my power to the wishes
of Government.

I have the honor to be,

Sir,

Your most obedient Servant,

(Signed) FRAMJI COWASJI.

Bombay, 17th December 1847.

No. 205/48

WILLIAM COURTNEY, Esquire,

Secretary to Government, Bombay.

Sir,

Having received no reply to my letter to the Hon'ble the
late Governor, Mr. Clerk, No. 279, dated the 17th December
1847, I beg to enclose herein a duplicate of the same, and
to request that you will kindly take an early opportunity
to submit it for the indulgent consideration of the Right
Hon'ble the Governor in Council.

Should His Lordship in Council not approve of the terms on which I have proposed to comply with the wish of the Hon'ble the Court of Directors that I should give up the Abkaree of the Poway Estate, I shall be happy to reconsider the matter with the Collector of Tanna or any other officer with whom Government may see fit to place me in communication on the subject.

I have the honor to be,

Sir,

Your most obedient servant,

(Signed)   FRAMJI COWASJI.

BOMBAY, 30th November 1848.

No 1752 of 1849.

TERRITORIAL DEPARTMENT, REVENUE.

To

FRAMJI COWASJI, ESQUIRE,

Bombay.

SIR,

I have laid before the Right Hon'ble the Governor in Council your letter No. 205 of the 30th November last, handing up the duplicate of one addressed by you to Government on the 17th December preceeding, in which you offer to relinquish the Abkaree of your Poway Estate in Salsette, for an annual Compensation of Rupees (25,000) twenty-five thousand.

2. In reply I have been instructed to state that the amount of Compensation demanded by you for the relinquishment of the Abkaree of your Estate, appears to his Lordship in Council, exorbitant and cannot be entertained.

3. The Government, I am to add, would be willing to make some sacrifice of Revenue with this object in view, but when, as appears from a report made by the Collector of Tanna, Rupees (2,000) two thousand per annum would be more than a fair equivalent, it cannot consent to give a sum equal to more than twelve times that amount.

I have the honor to be,

Sir,

Your most obedient servant,

(Signed) W. COURTNEY,

Acting Secretary to Government.

BOMBAY CASTLE, 10th March 1849.

No. 449 of 1855.

GENERAL DEPARTMENT.

To

BAEE BACHOOBAEE,

Widow of FRAMJI COWASJI, Esq.

MADAM,

I am directed by the Right Hon'ble the Governor in Council to communicate to you and to your Family, the great regret with which he had learnt, that the principal part of the large Country House at Poway, belonging to your late husband, was destroyed by fire on the 14th instant.

I am, Madam,

Your obdient Servant,

(Signed) W. HART,

Secretary to Government.

BOMBAY CASTLE, 31st January 1855.

WILLIAM HART, Esquire,

Secretary to Government,

General Department.

Sir,

I have the honor to acknowledge the receipt of your letter of the 31st ultimo, and in reply I beg you will be good enough to convey to His Lordship in Council the deep sense of gratitude I owe to His Lordship for the very kind and benevolent manner in which his Lordship in Council has shown his sympathy with me and my family on the occasion of the unfortunate occurrence we have met with by the recent destruction by fire of the principal part of the Country House of my late husband at Poway, and with sentiments of my sincere and heart-felt thanks to His Lordship for the same.

I have the honor to be,

Sir,

Your most obedient servant,

(Sd.) BUCHOOBAEE, Widow and Executrix
of the late Framji Cowasji by her
Attorney, Cursetji Nusserwanji Cama.

Bombay, 3rd February 1855.

CHAPTER XIII.

The Framji Cowasji Testim·nial.

Pursuant to notice published in the Newspapers, a number of the Friends of the late Framji Cowasji, Esq., met at the Elphinstone College, 22nd September 1852, to consider the fittest mode of applying the sums which have been raised by subscription to perpetuate his memory. The Chair was occupied by P. W. LeGeyt, Esq.

Among those who attended the Meeting we observed the following :—

The Hon'ble Sir E. Perry, Colonel Shortt, Dr. Morehead, Professor Patton, Captain French, Gregor Grant, Esq., Dr. Peet, G. H. Walker, Esq., Manockjee Limjee, Fsq., Juggonath Sunkersett, Esq., Cursetjee Jamsetjee, Fsq., Bomanjee Hormusjee, Esq., Narrayen Dinnanathjee, Esq., Rustomjee Jamsetjee, Fsq., Venaikerao Vassoodeo, Esq., Venaikrao Jaggonath, Esq., Bappoo Josey Rao Bahadoor, Hormusjee Bamanjee, Esq., Nowrojee Furdonjee, Esq., Rustomjee Ruttonjee, Esq., Sorabjee Ruttonjee, Esq., Sorabjee Pestonjee, Esq., Jamsetjee Cooverjee, Fsq., Dosabhoy Sorabjee Moonshee, Ruttonjee Furdoonjee Parruck, Vurjeevandas Maddowdas, Esq., and Framjee Nusservanjee Patell, Esq.

A number of Native gentlemen, among whom we observed all the grandsons of the late Framji Cowasji, Esq., and a large number of the Scholars of the Elphinstone Insitution headed by the Assistant Professor Dadabhai Nowrojee.

P. W. LeGeyt, Esquire, the Chairman, commenced the business of the Meeting with the following address :—

GENTLEMEN,—We have met here to-day to pay respect to the memory of a very estimable and remarkable man, who has lately been taken away from us by death. You have done me the honor to put me in the Chair on this intersting occasion ; and although I could have wished this office to have been confiled to some better and abler hands, yet a friendship of thirty years with the late Framji Cowasji, give me the privilege of considering myself one of the oldest is not the oldest of his European friends in the Presidency. Framji Cowasji was so well known to all of us, that it would be superfluous to usher in these proceedings by any sketch of his character and career ; but it will be more appropriate in this place to read to you a short extract from the Report of the Board of Education, of which he was long a distinguished member, notifying to Government his resignation of his seat at the Board ; and of the reply of Government conveying its opinion of his eminent and valuable services. The Board express themselves as follows in the second paragraph of their report, dated the 29th May 1851.

" At a later period in the year, Framji Cowasji, Esquire, resigned his seat, in consequence of his advanced time of life, and the vacancy was filled up by the election of Bomanjee Hormusjee, Esquire. The eminent and good citzenship, and zeal in supporting every measures for public improvement, which distinguished our late much esteemed colleague, are too well known to your Lordship in Council to need any notice from us ; but in recording his death, which subsequently occurred at the good old age of eightyfour, the Board feel a melancholy pleasure in thus publicly expressing the respect in which they hold his memory." The reply of Government to this notice is contained in the forty-fourth paragraph of Mr. Secretary Lumsden's letter No. 3480, dated the 6th September 1851 and is as follows:— " In conclusion, I am instructed to observe, that the tribute which the Board have paid in the second paragraph of their Report, to the late Framji Cowasji, Esquire, has been very properly rendered on this occasion to the memory of an excellent and deserving man. The Right Honorable the Governor in Council gladly avails himself of this opportunity again to express the high opinion entertained by himself and his predecessors of the worth of the deceased, as one who perceived that he could best serve his country by encouraging education, and who acted up to his persuation." The Chairman resumed his address as follows :—These sentiments, Gentlemen, are, I am sure, fully concurred in by this meeting, and by a large portion of the community of Bombay, which has been abundantly proved by the ready way in which the proposal to perpetuate Framji Cowasji's memory was received by all classes of people. This is the first instance that has been known in which persons of the classes and denominations (Natives and Europeans) have come forward to raise posthumous Testimonial in honor of a Native of this Presidency. Professor Patton will explain to you immediately the nature of the Memorial which it is proposed to erect; and I think you will agree with me, that it is a very appropriate one considering that Framji Cowasji's intelligent and active mind was ever alive to the improvement of his countrymen, and he was very constantly foremost in proposing measures for their mental culture and moral improvement. Witness too his many charities, his zeal for the spiritual welfare of his tribe, while the Dhobies' Tank and the reservoir on the Obelisk Road, to which water is conducted from an estate in Girgaum, the produce of which he set apart to secure a permanent supply of water to the public—betokens that his benevolence was not limited to the community of which he was a member. These good works, completed in his lifetime, will doubtless be constantly remembered by a greatful community ; but the present Testimonial, of which I am certain he would himself have highly approved, will in a peculiar manner in after ages perpetuate his memory, and bring forth the virtues of that good man constantly before your children and your children's grand-children. Such is the nature of the Testimonial to be pro-posed to your consideration, and I commend it to your adoption as members of an intelligent and enlightened community. *Great Applause.*

The following resolution was then propossed by *Juggonath Sunkersett, Esq.,* and seconded by Captain French.

Resolved,—That this meeting entertaining a high sense of the value of the services of the late Framji Cowasji, Esquire, to the cause of intellectual and social improvements in the country, are anxious to perpetuate his name in con-nection with some useful object which he would have approved.

Professor Patton was the next speaker, he said :—

Mr. Chairman and Gentlemen,—Before deciding upon the means of carrying out the previous Resolution, we ought to weigh well the consequences of this day's determination. This is not an ordinary occasion : it is the first time, as far as I am aware, that people of all classes have united in their desire to erect a testimonial to a native of this country. I hope and believe that many similar meetings will be held to commemorate the sterling honesty and public spirit of many others equally deserving. In fact there is one amongst us that it would be impossible to pass over even if he lived in a nation of Howards. Looking forward then to the future, and remembering that the decision of this day will influence the appropriation of testimonials long after we ourselves shall have ceased to influence anything, let us give a precedent we shall be delighted to see followed on other occasions. You have already decided upon the test by which the merits of any proposed scheme must be tried. It must

be such as would have received the approbation of the
worthy man whose name we have this day met to commemorate. I do not know of any better that could have
been adopted, for every thing which had for its object to
improve the condition of this country, either intellectually,
morally or physically, was approved of by him and received
from him support as far as in his power. I am satisfied
that the proposal I am about to make, unites every requisite
to secure your approbation. It is good in itself, and would
have received the approbation of the late Framji Cowasji.
But I shall first read the Resolution.

" That the funds which have been already collected, and
such others as may be subsequently added, be appropriated to
the formation of a Museum in connection with the Students'
Literary and Scientific Society, and that this meeting unite
with them in requesting Government to erect a building to
contain a Lecture room, a Laboratory, Museum of Arts and
Industry, and library, and to permit the building to be
called the Framji Cowasji Institute."

This mode of commemorating the name of Framji
seems to be peculiarly appropriate. When the Students'
Literary and Scientific Society was in its infancy, and when
many friends of education were either cold or unfavourable
to it Framji Cowasji came forward and shewed his
approval of their plans and objects, by presenting a number
of lamps which he heard they required for their meetings.
This first gift to the Society was the commencement of
many others, and to the day of his death he took a warm
interest in all their proceedings. During his long career
(as you have heard detailed to-day) he was always foremost
in every efforts to extend education in this country, and his
views of what education ought to be, were characterised by
an elevation, and at the same a practicality, that could

scarcely have been expected from the imperfect education
he himself had received. He was one of the chief contributors to the erection of the building in which we are now
assembled, and which has, as was anticipated, risen to the
rank of a College. Nearly a quarter of a century ago,
when the Native community of Bombay met to consider
the most appropriate method of attesting their affectionate
and respectful sentiments towards the Hon'ble Mountstuart
Elphinstone, Framji Cowasji in a speech replete with
good sense and sound views, which in our testimonial-giving
age might be worthy of attention, proposed that the most
satisfactory and durable plan of carrying their wishes into
effect, was to found one or two professorships for teaching
the English language, the Arts, Science and Literature of
Europe. The Students' Literary and Scientific Society is
the direct result of that education, and a proof of the
wisdom and foresight that suggested it.

The education they have received at the Elphinstone
College enables them, and their own actively benevolent disposition prompts them, to spread among their less fortunate
countrymen the benefits that they themselves have enjoyed.
An enumeration of a few things that have been accomplish-
ed during the three years in which the Society has been
in existence, will enable you to appreciate the importance
of having the Testimonial attached to a Society of active
working men, who will go on adding to its value and importance—instead of allowing it, as most other schemes in
this country never fail to do—to become useless when its
original promoters are taken away. There is once a month
a meeting for transaction of business and reading essays in
English once a fortnight there are two meetings for a
similar purpose in the vernacular. At these vernacular
meetings large and interested audiences assemble, to see the
experiments and illustrations exhibited. Seven Girls'

schools at present containing...children are supported by the Society, and three Boys' infant schools containing .. boys, although supported by others, are under the superintendence of the Society. Two school books in Marathi and Guzerati have been already printed, and a third is ready for the press. Two monthly publications are issued by the vernacular branches, and the Society has lately undertaken to publish a series of papers in Marathi and Guzerati similar to Chambers' Information for the people. For this they have peculiar advantages having obtained from Messrs. Chambers stereotypes of the illustrations of their educational course. A commencement has also been made of a Library and Museum of Art and Industry, and many valuable contributions have been received. The great difficulty with which the Society is now labouring is the insufficient accommodation for lectures and the want of a place to deposit the donation of books and Philosophical apparatus, and donations of various kinds which are presented to them. The Society has applied to Government to assist them in this difficulty, and strong hopes are entertained that something will be done ; but if an influential meeting like the present gave their support to the application, and offer to grant the fund now collected for the testimonial to Framji Cowasji, to establish a Museum on the simple condition, that the building should be called the Framji Cowasji Institute. There can scarcely be a doubt that Government would erect a suitable building for the use of the Society.

I believe that the motion of this Institute will be an era on the Educational history of Bombay. It will give that prominence to the study of Physical science which this age demands, and which is so essentially required by the genius of the people and the want of the country. The experiments of Natural Philosophy will have much greater influence in disturbing the apathy that has reigned here for ages, and in creating a taste for reading, than any purely abstract speculations however beautiful. In the proposed Institute the artisan will see improved machines and improved tools for making them, while at the same time he will have an opportunity of learning the Mathematical and physical principles, without a knowledge of which they could never have been invented. The student who has learned the principles in the classroom, will there see the practical results they have led to and be brought to view in a proper light the dignity of labour. It is useless to detain you with a detailed account of the benefits that may be expected to Bombay from the proposed Institute, for you must be aware of them yourself; but I would wish to draw your attention to another important advantage that might be taken of it, in the dissemination of knowledge in the Mofussil. During vacations at the College such instruments as would not be likely to suffer injury, might be sent to the various large towns throughout the Presidency, and courses of lectures might be delivered that would have immense influence in destroying prejudice and superstition, and giving more elevated ideas of the nature of education than now prevail. I shall now conclude by proposing that—

" Funds which have been already collected and others as may be subsequently added, be appropriated to the formation of a Museum, in connection with " The Students' Literary and Scientific Society ;" and that this Meeting unite with them in requesting Government to erect a building to contain a lecture-room, laboratory, and to permit the building to be called " The Framji Cowasji Institute."

The Hon'ble SIR E. PERRY seconded this resolution in the following terms :

I have been requested to second this resolution ; and tired as I am, having been sitting in Court many hours to-day, I cannot be silent upon the subject of it. You, as his friend and as our colleague, Mr. Chairman, know how highly I estimated the character of our deceased friend (cheers). He was not a Scholar, and for the last ten years of his life he was not a wealthy man : indeed he had fallen into evil days, and yet he managed to secure the esteem and love of all who came within his influence ; and the question which suggests itself is—what were the qualities which won the esteem and love which he possessed of all the inhabitants of Bombay ? His eminent good citizenship. He possessed that virtue, not common among people now, in an eminent degree. It is a virtue too little exemplified by our Hindoo friends,—who I hope will excuse me for so saying ;—nor is it universal among the Parsees, but it is more so among them than among other classes. Framji Cowasji exercised that virtue more than others of his countymen : he was a steady good citizen, bold enough to speak out his opinion, and energetic to exert himself to do his country good. These virtues we are desirous to see universal. Having said so much, it will naturally be a matter of wonder to some of my Native friends—how is it that I figure so humbly in the subscription list to this Testimonial. It is a question which may well be asked, and I will assign the reason. For years past I have had a very great aversion to these testimonials : they have been carried too far, so as to appear ridiculous in the eyes of Society generally. They have usually been given to public men,—official men ; and as a point of Policy I should much like to see the system of presenting these testimonials abolished. I have often thought that it would be better if the rule which prevails in the Army with respect to the presentation of testimonials to Officers there, should be extended to Civil Society and that it should be neither careful for them to accept, nor decorous for Society to present them with such testimonials. Though I have subscribed, and not niggardly, to every testimonial which has been promulged, I held back when this was proposed ; and that is the reason, why the sum opposite my name in the list appears so insignificant. On reflection I think that in this instance I was wrong ; because the arguments I have alleged as leading me to think disparagingly of the system of presenting testimonials generally, do not apply to the individual to honour whose memory the present testimonials is proposed ; and when I to-day heard the objects aimed at by it recounted, I felt convinced that I was so ; and I feel myself called upon by a strong sense of approbation of those objects, to say how very desirous I am to see them fully realised.

Our friend the Chairman has read a highly eulogistic notice of the late Framji Cowasji and his services ; and we have heard what a deep interest he took in the proceedings of these young men who have formed themselves into a Society for the object of conferring benefits upon their countrymen. It will, I am sure, be gratifying to them, and to Professor Patton who has gone hand in hand with them in all their efforts, to hear what Government says upon the subject. I catch the eye of one young man who especially, I know, will be gratified to hear this eulogium :—

" The voluntary association of the educated youth of Bombay for the purpose of instructing their countrymen, and of bringing all within their influence justly appreciate the advantages of education, is very gratifying to Government, as it is honourable to the parties concerned.

" In particular, the spontaneous institutions, by the same youngmen of Female Schools, which they also entirely support, must be regarded as an epoch in the history of education at this Presidency, from which it is to be hoped will in due time be traced the commencement of a rapid, marked, and constant progress.

That is strong language from the Government of the Presidency, my friends. When we hear of the friends of that man proposing a plan in honor of his memory, whereby the Society of these young men may gain "a local habitation and a name,"—which will give them far more extended opportunities for the diffusion of science, for the reception and collection of Scientific objects, and a place of accommodation for the truth-seeking, self-instructing classes of the Native community ;—when we hear of a proposal like this, it must command our admiration. There is one particular feature in this matter to which, if this is to be considered the inauguration of the building and the institute, I must call attention. In those efforts which have been made by the young men of Bombay for the diffusion of knowledge and science, they have been assisted liberally and gladly by the elder portion of the community. This is not usually the case in ordinary undertakings and projects ; and it is a very satisfactory phenomenon,—youth and age consorted together in the most useful and honorable occupation which could be pursued by them. We cannot but look upon this with admiration. There is a tendency in the hearts of youth to become inflated, and a desire to throw off their obedience to the just authority which belongs to those who are older in life and riper in experience than themselves. It is, therefore, a complimentary homage to the individual to honour whom this Institute has been set on foot—that the elders of Society come forward so graciously, and unite hand in hand with the younger and more ardent members of Society for the advancement of their measures.

As I before said, my apathy to subscribe to this testimonial was a mistake on my part, or the argument I gave for any aversion to testimonials in general did not apply to this case ; and I have expressed as forcibly as I can, my approbation of the scheme proposed to perpetuate the memory of Framji Cowasji. But it behoves us to act as well as to talk; and I therefore beg that the Secretary will add another " 0 " to the figures opposite my name in the subscription List.

I have great pleasure in seconding this Resolution.

Assistant Professor D idabhoy Nowrojee said :—

GENTLEMEN,—I have the pleasure to lay before you a proposal from the "Students' Literary and Scientific Society," that the Society would be most happy in availing themselves of this opportunity, to express their esteem of the worthy dead, whose name we have here assembled to commemorate in some way. Professor Patton at some length gave reasons for establishing a new Institution, the like of which has yet had no existence, in this Presidency at least, and perhaps not in the whole of India ; and which he has endeavoured to show would have been most approved of by Framji himself.

The Students' Society therefore, being in many ways indebted to Framji's support and benevolence, lays at the disposal of this Committee the sum of Rupees 6,000, that they have been able to collect, for providing the Branch Societies (or the Dnanprasaracs especially) with the means of fully illustrating the lectures delivered by the students of this Institution to hundreds of their own countrymen. This object, the Society see, will be more fully gained by an amalgamation of the two funds. The advantage likely to accrue to natives from the kind of Institution now contemplated to be established, are so many, that I could scarcely feel myself competent to give a detailed description of them all, I might at least say, that if the Students' Society and its Branches, with its very limited pecuniary me ns, but I am proud to say both the zeal and efforts of some of our best young men of this Institution, as its service, has been able to do something towards the diffusion of useful knowledge among the masses around it. It could be easily conceived, what the same zeal and efforts could do with better, I should rather say, more powerful means at its command. It has been often complained that English was taught to too many and that the price of service in offices had fallen very low. But it is no wonder that such should be the case—an overstocked market can never call forth high prices ; and why it is asked should every body be quill-driver, and why should it be more difficult to find a hamal than a clerk. The reason as I have already said, is very obvious : new opening must surely be made for the rising generation, and where are they to be looked for. Is India incapable of giving, at the least, a comfortable living to its children? No,—India has plenty, but how could that plenty be availed. Can a stone cry out and say : here am I, make use of me. Such and such are my properties, and such and such are the uses to which I am capable of being applied? No, that it cannot do,—and yet it may be perhaps the fruitful source of the happiness of millions. And if it is the lot of man to live by the sweat of his brow, to depend but upon the material world around him, and when he has at the same time given him the power of supplying the demands implanted in him by nature, it rests with him alone to apply those powers, and to labour till he can find out what he requires. This very Institution that is now proposed to be erected would be nothing but a mere pile of dead matter, if it be not animated by the labor and energy of active men. The inference is clear enough, that man can find nothing that he does not seek for, and that in a proper way. India has plenty, and that plenty must be sought, and under a particular condition —labour, by great and impresuming, but well applied, labour of those competent to perform the task. I congratulate on this occasion the Inhabitants of Bombay at least, that that same Framji Cowasji, to whom, with some others, and to him whose name this Institution bears, they are at this moment indebted for the advancement of education and sounder principles among them, is at the same time the founder of a new Institution suited to their present increased wants. Have not the people of India been impressed with the conviction, that its present arts are capable of being immensely improved and increased in number? We have a proof of this conviction in this very worthy man. Need I describe here the trouble he put himself to, and the liberality with which he left his purse always open for any useful purpose to introduce improvement in agriculture and even introduce new arts in India. If then the young men of the Students' Society—furnished with the means of studying most of the useful arts, manufactures, be able to promulgate their knowledge in a practical form, by means of lectures to hundreds; what could be thought more useful to the count y, whose good was, to his, Framji's heart. Imagine to yourself gentlemen, a Hall with 500 men collected in it, a young lecturer, ready to impart with a good grace and feeling, the results of his some days' labour at the furnace. Let me next carry you out of the Hall, an enterprising listener takes up the idea, consults the lecturer again, and in time becomes a blessing to the community around him,—introduces, practices a new art, and thus makes a new opening for the industrious, and gives the world the lesson afresh—that the industrious shall never starve, a lesson more valuable than anything else. Imagine gentlemen again, another reading to the assembly a lesson on some of the principal moral duties of man, claiming by his earnest exhortations some heart gone astray—persuading with true vehemence to abandon a pernicious custom, or giving more homely, but not the less useful lessons, such as that "Honesty is the best policy;" and a third, exhorting to emulate Newton or Watt; or to use the more simple and more expressive words of Framji himself,—" to be able to count the very stars of Heaven." How often did he say, I am told " these men must be taught anything good and ennobling; they must be taught every thing, they must be taught to count even the stars of Heaven." If such results indeed be very desirable, and were at least so heartily desired by the worthy man to be commemorated, what better means could be suggested, than be enabled to adopt the most natural course of furnishing those with adequate means that have the will, and the ability to bring them about. If such there be now, mere halls indeed can do nothing; but the very demand that has now arisen for such an Institution speaks loudly—that the labourers are not wanting; and it is a matter of great congratulation, that the supply is forthcoming, as soon as the demand is made and felt, and more particularly because, from the same quarter to which we when young owe a great deal. It might perhaps have been expected that, it would descant upon the many virtues, high spirit, and straightforwardness of Framji, but it is a matter already so ably dealt with by persons competent to do it deserving justice, that I should blush to venture to say a word upon the subject. Yet I cannot refrain myself from expressing my sentiments towards this worthy man. I have had but once for all a talk with him, but the impression that that single visit made upon me and my friend Ardaseer, shall never wear off. It was for the purpose of asking support to our Female schools; and how could I now describe a scene that could only be seen. Yet I shall try. We approached with great trepidation, knew not what should be the result of the visit, for we knew not the man, and it was our first visit. But Framji shewed that he was always prepared to receive even a child with pleasure that brought good tidings of any kind. Many were the sound advices he gave us as to our conduct in the undertaking, many hopes did he raise in us, and shewed great concern that he could not stretch out as good an helping hand than as he was wont to do before. His advices, however, were more worth than anything else, and we have now the opportunity of expressing our obligations for the benefit with which we followed those advices: trifling as they might often appear, they are the forerunners of great things to come. Trifling as the Table Lamp present made to the Society might appear, it was the kindler of the first spark of hope, that an earnest desire and endeavour to do an useful thing shall never fail to be properly appreciated. For any body however to say all that could be said upon so tempting a subject, requires the study of the life of that eminent man. That study however nobody is prepared to make, and nobody can do all the justice that it deserves ; much less therefore can I pretend to say all, I must therefore stop, and only perform the pleasing task assigned me, by repeating, that the Students' Society have directed me to intimate, that they would be most happy to add to the sum already subscribed to the Framji Cowasji Testimonial, the sum of Rs. 6,000 which they have raised up for purposes similar to that which is now proposed to be carried out.

The following motion was then proposed by Cursetjee Jamsetjee, Esq., seconded by Manockjee Limjee, Esq., and passed,—

" That the following gentlemen be elected to form a Committee to communicate with Government on the subject, and to make such arrangements as may be considered most expedient to carry out the wishes of the meeting.

Mr. Warden, Mr. LeGeyt, Mr. Cursetjee Jamsetjee, Dr. McLennan, Mr. Juggonath Sunkersett, Captain French,

Mr. Bomanjee Hormusjee, Mr. Manockjee Limjee, Mr. Howard, Mr. McKenzie, Mr. Manockjee Cursetjee, Mr. Cowie, Mr. Patton, Mr. Narrayen Dinanathjee, Mr. Cursetjee Nusserwanjee Cama, Mr. Dadabhoy Nowrojee, Mr. Sorabjee Pestonjee Framjee and Mr. Rustomjee Jamsetjee.

The fourth resolution was proposed by Bomonjee Hormusjee, Esq., seconded by Mr. Manockjee Cursetjee, " That a marble slab with an appropriate inscription in English, Guzerattee and Marathee, be erected in the Institute, to perpetuate the memory of the late Framji Cowasji, Esq.

The following is Mr. SORABJEE PESTONJEE's address.

MR. CHAIRMAN AND GENTLEMEN,—Before the proceedings of this meeting are concluded, I trust you will allow me to speak a few words, and with your permission, I shall at once proceed to read the paper in my hand.

As it has fallen to my lot, Gentlemen, I rise to speak in behalf of my old grandmother, and the other members of the family of my reverend and lamented grandfather, the late Framji Cowasji, to commemorate whose name you have raised a fund, and have met here this day to adopt the best means of appropriating that money. His friends and the community who have shown their kind intentions of thus perpetuating the memory of the deceased gentleman, must have felt his loss; but it is with extreme pain I say, that his loss to the family has been greater, for in him we have lost a kind patron, a beloved and the most affectionate of fathers, and the protector of many orphans, and widows,—his loss, therefore, shall ever remain engraved on our hearts as long as we live. The severity of the afflictions of his aged widow, can be better imagined than described; but she was not the less gratified when she heard that her husband's name was about to be perpetuated by a suitable testimonial from his friends and countrymen. Indeed this

has proved a very great consolation to her, as she is convinced that her dear companion did not (to use the Persian
saying) come into the world and go away without doing
anything. As to his deeds and how praiseworthy they
may be, I will not take upon myself to enter into particulars, although I have had ample opportunities of witness-
ing many of them ; for however strong my voice may be in
his favor, it would not sound so well and so gracefully as
your's would. Moreover, our worthy Chairman, from his
long acquaintance with the career of life of the deceased, as
well as the Hon'ble the Chief Justice, and the other gentlemen who have preceded me, have already said enough about
his character, and who have, I have no doubt, left a sufficient impression upon your minds, of the desirableness of
thus publicly appreciating the good services, which the
decesased gentleman rendered to his fellow countrymen. It
is the duty of every man, if it lay in his power to assist and
devise means for the good of his fellow creatures, and it was
with these pure and honest motives that the deceased
devoted himself during his long life to do some service to his
countrymen. And as deserving merits have never failed
to meet with due reward, I am glad, nay proud to find, that
for the little good the deceased may have been able to do
while in the performance of his duties towards his fellow
brethren, he is held in such high estimation in the eyes of
you all, and that such a mark of tribute is paid by you to
his departed life. This does not only preserve the name of
the deceased, but also bestows a great and an everlasting
honor on us, his descendants, should we be so fortunate as
to follow his footsteps. Allow me therefore, Gentlemen, to
express to you in behalf of the old lady my grandmother,
my father, and the other members of the family, allow me
so to express their sincere and grateful thanks to you all,
and to those Gentlemen individually who have since his

death, showed a great desire to perpetuate his memory. With regard to the object to which you have now resolved, Gentlemen, to appropriate the fund, I am happy to say it is just the very thing which the deceased Gentleman had always in his heart. For I remember well he often expressed his earnest desire to make arrangements to teach the Students of this noble Institution every branch of knowledge, such as to use his own words, the science of calculating the movements of the stars, that is Astronomy, Navigation, and other similar sciences, his desire therefore is now, I am glad to say, about to be fulfilled by the hands of you his friends, and I trust that the " Framji Cowasji Institute " will henceforth prove to be a school for the advancement of the Students of the Elphinstone Institution, and through their medium it will, I venture to hope, be a source for diffusing scientific, useful knowledge among the natives of this country. And in conclusion, I hope and pray that the projectors of this Institution may be blessed with every success in their best intended endeavours.

Thanks were then returned to the Chairman for his able conduct in the Chair, and the meeting broke up at half-past six o'clock.

CHAPTER XIV.

Correspondence with Government, the Collector of Land Revenues, the Director of Public Instruction and the Municipal Commissioners, on the subject of the Framji Cowasji Institute.

No. 4577 of 1851.

GENERAL DEPARTMENT.

To

JOSEPH PATTON, ESQUIRE,

Secretary to the Committee of the

Framji Cowasji Testimonial.

SIR,

I have been directed by the Right Honorable the Governor in Council to acknowledge the receipt of your letter dated the 21st November last, submitting certain Resolutions passed at a late meeting of the subscribers to the Framji Cowasji Testimonial, and soliciting the aid of Government towards establishing a Museum in connection with the Students' Literary and Scientific Society.

2. The Government of India, have recently declined to sanction an allowance of Rupees (150) one hundred and fifty per mensem, solicited by the Students' Literary and Scientific Society, to meet the expense of a Building suitable for the purposes of a Library, Lecture Room, and Laboratory, on the ground that that Institution was not of a nature to warrant such a grant to it from the Public Revenues.

3 This Resolution of the Government of India is equally applicable to the present request. The usefulness of the Students' Literary and Scientific Institution has nowhere been more fully acknowledged than by the Govern-

m2nt, and it is therefore with the greater regret that His Lordship in Council is compelled to refuse the Committee's application.

I have the honor to be,
Sir,
Your most obedient Servant,
(Signed)   A. RICHARDSON,
Deputy Secry. to Govt.

BOMBAY CASTLE, 20th December 1851.

To
J. G. LUMSDEN, ESQUIRE,
Secretary to Government,
General Department.

SIR,

I have the honor to acknowledge the receipt of a letter from A. Richardson, Esquire, Acting Secretary to Government, intimating that the Government of India had refused to sanction an allowance of Rs 150 per month, to the Students' Literary and Scientific Society for house rent, and that the Honorable the Governor in Council conceived a similar reply would be given to an application which I had the honor to submit on behalf of the Committee of the Framji Cowasji Testimonial. In reply, I would take the liberty of stating, that the sum now collected for the Framji Cawasji Testimonial, amounts to nearly Rs. 10,000, and that there is not much hope of increasing this considerably. With this sum the Committee cannot carry out, even imperfectly, the plans which they had in contemplation, and they earnestly request that Government taking into consideration the worth of Framji Cowasji in honor of whom the Testimonial has been proposed, and the highly useful labours of the Students' Literary and Scientific Society for whom the building is intended together with the general advantages to be expected from the Library, Lectures, and Museum, will grant a piece of ground for a building, and make such a donation to the fund as will enable the Committee to erect a building suitable for the purposes proposed.

I have the honor to be,

Sir,

Your most obedient Servant,

(Sd.) JOSEPH PATTON, Secy. to the Committee.

Elphinstone Institution, Bombay, 7th February 1852.

No. 578 of 1852.

GENERAL DEPARTMENT.

To
    J. PATTON, Esquire,
        Secretary to the Framji Cowasji
            Testimonial Committee.

Sir,

I am directed to acknowledge the receipt of your letter, dated the 7th instant, and in reply to acquaint you, that as a mark of the approbation with which the Right Honorable the Governor in Council regards the exertions made by the members of the Literary and Scientific Society to promote the education of their countrymen, he is pleased to grant a donation of Rs. 4,000 to be added to the Fund of Rs. 10,000 which has been collected for the purpose of erecting a Museum, &c.

2. The decision of Government on the request of the Committee that Government will grant them a piece of ground as a site for the proposed building will be separately disposed of and communicated to you hereafter.

I have the honor to be,

Sir,

Your most obedient Servant,

(Signed) J. G. LUMSDEN, Secy. to Govt.

BOMBAY CASTLE, *28th February* 1852.

To

J. W. MUSPRATT, Esquire,

General Paymaster.

Sir,

I have the honor to write to you that in a letter No. 578 of 1852, dated the 28th February 1852, addressed by J. G. Lumsden, Esq., Secretary to Government, to my predecessor the late Professor Patton, it was intimated to him that the Right Honorable the Governor in Council was pleased to grant a donation of Rs. 4,000 to be added to the Framj Cowasji Testimonial Fund. I beg therefore to request you will have the goodness to pay the amount to the bearer, whom I have authorized to receive it and pass a receipt for ·the same.

I have the honor to be,

Sir,

Your most obedient Servant,

NARAYEN DINANATHJI,

BOMBAY, 18th January 1853. Acting Secretary.

No. 276 of 1852.

MEMORANDUM.

The officer in charge Land Revenue Collector's office presents compliments to Professor Patton, and with reference to the subjoined copy of a Memo : from Mr. Secretary Lumsden, No. 2635, dated the 16th instant, begs the favor of Professor Patton informing him, whether he has as yet made any selection of the ground which he was informed might be made over to the Committee of the Framji Cowasji Testimonial.

A. D. ROBERTSON,

In charge Land Revenue Collector's Office.

BOMBAY COLLECTOR'S OFFICE, 21st July 1852.

To
A. D. ROBERTSON, ESQUIRE,
Acting Collector, Land Revenue in Bombay.

SIR,

I have the honor to inform you that the Committee of the Framji Cowasji Testimonial have appointed P. W. LeGeyt, Esq., Dr. McLenan, Juggunnath Sunkersett, Esq., and me, to make a selection of one of the pieces of ground offered them by Government, and that these gentlemen having resolved to meet at the country house of Juggunnath Sunkersett, Esq., on the Breach Road, at 5 o'clock P.M., on Monday, the 13th instant, and to proceed thence to examine the pieces of ground, you have been requested to send your Deputy Surveyor or any other person you may think proper to meet them at the above mentioned place at the appointed time, and to give them any information they may require respecting the spots in question.

I have the honor to be,
Sir,
Your most obedient Servant,
(Signed) NARAYEN DINANATHJI,
BOMBAY, 8th September 1852.   Acting Secretary.

No. 357 OF 1852.

From
A. D. ROBERTSON, ESQUIRE,
In charge Land Revenue Collector's Office,

To
NARAYEN DINANATHJI, ESQUIRE,
Acting Secretary.

SIR,

In reply to your letter of this day's date, I beg to inform you, that I have given orders for a Surveyor to be in attendance on the gentlemen appointed by the Committee of

the Framji Cowasji Testimonial to select a piece of ground
on the evening of the 13th instant, at the house of Juggunnath Sunkersett, Esq.

I have the honor to be,
Sir,
Your most obedient Servant,
A. D. ROBERTSON,
In charge Land Revenue, Collector's Office.
BOMBAY, COLLECTOR'S OFFICE, 8th September 1852.

No. 191 of 1853.

MEMORANDUM

The Collector of Bombay presents his compliments to
the Secretary to the Com-
mittee of the Framji Cowasji
Testimonial, and begs to be
informed, with reference to
the correspondence noted in
the margin, whether the committee have made any selection
of the ground which they propose to ask Government to
make over to them for the Framji Cowasji Testimonial.

1. Memo. from Mr. Robertson,
Officiating Collecter to Professor
Patton, dated 21st July 1852.
2 Mr. Acting Secretary Nara-
yon Dinanathji's letter to Mr Robertson, dated 8th September 1852.
3. Mr. Robertson's Reply No. 357,
dated 8th September 1852.

F. HUTCHINSON, Collector.

BOMBAY, COLLECTOR'S OFFICE, 17th May 1853.

No. 111 OF 1854.

To
NARAYEN DINANATHJI, ESQUIRE,
Secretary to the Committee of the
Framji Cowasji Testimonial.

SIR,
With reference to your letter of the 16th ultimo, I have
the honor to request that you will be good enough to inform me what has been done in respect to the selection of a
piece of ground for the Framji Cowasji Testimonial.

2. I beg an early answer, which is required to enable me to reply to a further reference which has been made to me by Government.

I have the honor to be,
Sir,
Your most obedient Servant,
F. HUTCHINSON, Collector.

BomBay, Collector's Office, 18*th March* 1854.

No. 237 of 1854.

To
NARAYEN DINANATHJI, Esquire,
Secretary to the Committee of the
Framji Cowasji Testimonial.

Sir,
Adverting to my letter of the 18th March last, to which I have yet received no reply, I have the honor to acquaint you that, I have received the instructions of Government to offer the Committee as a site for the proposed Testimonial, one of the spots of ground on the verge of the Esplanade, which were made over to several parties in 1836 on sufference tenure and of which a plan may be seen in this office.

2. I request you will be good enough to inform me with as little delay as possible, which of those spots the Committee would wish to have for that purpose.

I have the honor to be,
Sir,
Your most obedient Servant,
F. HUTCHINSON, Collector.

BomBay, Collector's Office, 26*th June* 1854.

To

F. HUTCHINSON, Esq.,

Collector of Land Revenue, Bombay.

SIR,

In reply to your letter No. 237 of 1854, dated the 26th June last, I have the honor to inform you by the direction of the Managing Committee of Framji Cowasji Institute, that they have chosen the spot marked 71 in your plan as a site for the proposed Institute, and shall feel obliged by your adopting early measures to put them in possession of it.

I have been further directed to inform you, that it is their intention to erect on the spot, an upper roomed building of the dimensions described in the accompanying plan.

The Committee observe, that a small piece of ground adjoining that selected by them is not to be obtained without compensating the tenants, I allude to the spot marked No. 43 in your plan. As it is essential that the Committee should be placed in possession of this piece of ground, I shall be obliged by your informing me the amount of compensation that will be required to obtain it.

I have the honor to be,

Sir,

Your most obedient Servant,

NARAYEN DINANATHJI, Secretary.

BOMBAY, 3rd August 1854.

No. 318 of 1854.

To

NARAYEN DINANATHJI, Esquire,

Secretary, Framji Cawasji Institute.

Sir,

With reference to the 3rd paragraph of your letter of the 3rd instant, I have the honor to state that the piece of ground therein alluded to belongs to Government and could be resumed, I think, by Government under the provisions of act XVII of 1850, I have made enquiry and find that the erections thereon, being tiled sheds used as shops, are the property of the persons named in the margin, whose aggregate rental therefrom is about Rupees eight hundred per annum. It is difficult to say what amount of Compensation would be awarded them by a Jury, but I have little doubt that the Committee might purchase the shops for less than the owner would expect from Government.

Munguldass Nuthoobhoy, Fuzloodin Nowruugay.

2. I beg to be informed at your earliest convenience whether the Committee desire the spot marked No. 71 in the plan shown to you in this office, for the Institute irrespectively of their obtaining or not the piece of adjoining ground above alluded to.

I have the honor to be,

Sir,

Your most obedient Servant,

F. HUTCHINSON, Collector.

BOMBAY, COLLECTOR's OFFICE, 18th August 1854.

No. 2739 of 1854.

GENERAL DEPARTMENT.

To
THE SECRETARY to THE FRAMJI COWASJI
TESTIMONIAL COMMITTEE, BOMBAY.

SIR,

With reference to paragraph 2nd of the letter from this department (No. 578), dated the 28th February, 1852, I am directed to refer the Committee to the Collector of Bombay, who has received the instructions of Government regarding the ground applied for.

I have the honor to be,
Sir,
Your most obedient Servant,
C. G. FRASER TYTLER,
Offg. Secretary to Govt.

BOMBAY CASTLE, 18th August 1854.

To
F. HUTCHINSON, ESQUIRE,
Collector of Land Revenue, Bombay.

SIR,

I have the honor to inform you, that the Committee of the Framji Cowasji Institute have instructed me to accept the spot No. 71 for the Institute leaving the question of obtaining the adjoining spot for future consideration and to request the favour of your putting them in possession of the spot as early as possible.

I have the honor to be,
Sir,
Your most obedient Servant,
NARAYEN DINANATHJI, Secretary.

BOMBAY, 7th September 1854.

No. 442 of 1854.

To

NARAYEN DINANATHJI, Esquire,

Secretary to the Framji Cowasji Institute.

Sir,

With reference to your letter of the 7th September last, I have the honor to inform you, that Government have intimated to me that the spot selected by the Committee cannot be made available for the purpose of the Institute.

I have the honor to be,

Sir,

Your most obedient Servant,

F. HUTCHINSON, Collector.

Bompay, Collector's Office, 22nd November 1854.

To

H. YOUNG, Esquire,

Officiating Chief Secretary to Government,

Bombay.

Sir,

I have the honor by desire of the Sub-Committee of the Framji Cowasji Institute to state for the information of his Lordship in Council, that some time ago they applied to Government for a piece of ground for the use of the Institute and Government was pleased to offer through the Collector of Bombay some of the spots on the verge of the Esplanade. The Committee thereupon selected one of them and intimated their determination to that officer, saguinely hoping, from two pressing letters addressed to them by that officer requesting them to come to an early determination in making their selection, that they would soon be put in possession of it, but the last letter of that officer intimated to the Committee, that the spot selected by them could not be made available for the purpose of the Institute.

Now the Committee beg again to bring to the notice of Government that the fund at their disposal is just sufficient for building and fitting up the proposed Institute and will hardly leave anything for the purchase of a piece of ground and they therefore earnestly request that Government, taking into consideration the worth of the late Framji Cowasji, Esq., in commemoration of whom the Institute has been proposed to be established and the useful labours of the Students' Literary and Scientific Society for whom the building is chiefly intended, as also the important advantages that the Native community in general will derive from the Library, Museum and Lectures in connection with the proposed Institute, will favour the Committee by complying with their request.

I have the honor to be,

Sir,

Your most obedient Servant,

NARAYEN DINANATHJI, Secretary.

BOMBAY, 22nd February 1855.

_____

To

W. HART, Esq.,

Officiating Chief Secretary to Government.

SIR,

With reference to my last letter to the address of your predecessor on the subject of a site for the Framji Cowasji Institute, I have the honor to state that having lately been in communication with the Collector of Bombay, I was given to understand that Government having permitted the heirs of the late Mahomed Ebrahim Muckba to retain on their payment to Government of a certain amount of valuation, the spot of ground on the verge of the Esplanade which the Committee of the Framji

Cawasjee had applied for, the spot in question could not be made available for the purpose of the Institute. I was further informed that there was no other piece of ground belonging to Government that would suit the purposes of the Institute.

Under these circumstances I have been directed by the Sub-Committee of the Framji Cowasji Institute to write to you, that as Government, having a due regard to the many excellent qualities of the individual in commemoration of whom the Institute is proposed to be founded as well as to the general usefulness of the Institute to the Natives at large, have kindly expressed their desire to provide the Committee with a piece of ground for the Institute and would have in fact given the piece of ground the Committee had applied for, had Government not shown an indulgent consideration to the claims to the ground of the heirs of the late Mahomed Ebrahim Muckba and as there is no other piece of Government ground available for the purpose, the Committee have no other alternative but most respectfully to lay that His Lordship in Council will kindly extend his support to the Institute so far as to make over to it a certain sum of money at least equal to which may be received by Government as the valuation of the spot of ground which they were prepared to give for the use of the Institue, in order to enable the Committee to purchase another piece of ground for the Institute in a suitable locality.

I have the honor to be,

Sir,

Your most obedient Servant,

NARAYEN DINANATHJI, Secretary.

BOMBAY, 15*th May* 1855.

No. 1795 of 1855.

To
THE SECRETARY to the FRAMJI COWASJI
INSTITUTE.

SIR,

In reply to your letter dated the 15th May 1855, I am directed by the Right Honorable the Governor in Council to request that you will have the goodness to point out to the Collector of Bombay the spot of ground which the Committee would wish to negotiate for, were a pecuniary grant made to them as requested, in order to enable that officer to report whether it would not be feasible to obtain it from the owner by exchange of Government ground elsewhere, instead of by a money payment.

I have the honor to be,
Sir,
Your most obedient Servant,
W. HART, Secretary to Government.

BOMBAY CASTLE, 25th May 1855.

No. 237 of 1855.

To
NARAYEN DINANATHJI, Esquire,
Secretary to Framji Cowasji Institute.

SIR,

With reference to the request made by me to you, on several occasions since the receipt by you of Mr. Secretary Hart's letter, No. 1795, dated the 25th ultimo, that you would be so good as to point out to me the piece of ground for the obtainment of which the Committee would wish me to negociate with the owner, I have the honor to beg that I may be informed, as early as possible whether the Committee have selected a site for the Institute, in order to enable me to submit a report which I have been directed to make to Government on the subject.

I have the honor to be,

Sir,

Your most obedient Servant,

F. HUTCHINSON, Collector.

BOMBAY, COLLECTOR's OFFICE, 22nd June 1855.

To

F. HUTCHINSON Esquire,

Collector of Bombay.

SIR,

With reference to Mr. Secretary Hart's letter No. 1795, dated the 25th of May last, and yours of the 22nd June and 11th July last, I have been directed by the Sub-Committee of the Framji Cowasji Institute to inform, that the following are the four spots of ground, one of which they would negotiate for, were a pecuniary grant made to them by Government as requested in their letter of the 13th of May last.

1. A piece of ground belonging to Mr. Tyebji Bhaeemeea situated on the Esplanade cross road and adjoining the Scotch Free Church. There are a number of small houses on this spot.

2. The spot of ground situated on the Girgaum road near Framji Cowasji Tank on which the present building of the Native General Library stands. It is owned by Mr. Chintoba Ramchundra Chapwalla.

3. Ditto Ditto. It belongs to the Estate of the late Ramchander Pondoosett.

4. A spot of ground with a building standing thereon belonging to   situated on the Girgaum road near the Fire Temple of the late Hormusji Bomonji Esquire.

I have the honor to be,
Sir,
Your most obedient Servant,
NARAYEN DINANATHJI, Secretary.

Bombay, 21st *July* 1855.

No. 1180 of 1856.

Bombay Office of the Director of Public Instruction, 26th *June* 1856.

To
The SECRETARY to the FRAMJI COWASJI
INSTITUTE.

Sir,

You informed me in the month of March last, that the total sum at the disposal of the Framji Cowasji Institute for building purposes is now about Rs. 16,000 exclusive of the Rs. 4,000 granted by Government in 1852.

2. Government have now agreed to expend on the purchase of a suitable site for the Institute, such a sum as may be necessary to secure an ample and convenient one—provided that the amount now required together with that formerly assigned, shall not together exceed the sum above quoted as the private capital of the Institute.

3. I have been authorized within this limit to conclude, in communication with the Committee, a final arrangement on this subject. I had hoped that you would have been able ere this to have pointed out an advantageous and available situation. Up to this time apparently you have not succeeded and all idea of purchasing the site originally contemplated has, I believe been abandoned,—may I beg that

you will consult the Committee on the subject without loss of time and let me know their wishes as soon as possible. I would suggest a reference if necessary to the Collector of Bombay.

4. I need hardly indicate the propriety of the Committee after this liberal concession by Government making a hearty effort to add considerably to their private resources. I am confident that an appeal on this ground to the friends of the respected gentleman after whom the Institute is named would be warmly responded to.

5. Will you kindly favor me with a plan of the proposed building.

I have the honor to be,
Sir,
Your most obedient Servant,
C. J. ERSKINE,
Director of Public Instruction.

To
E. I. HOWARD, Esq.,
Director of Public Instruction, Bombay.

Sir,
With reference to your letter No. 904 of 1857, dated the 23rd May 1857, I have been instructed by the Sub-Committee of the Framji Cowasji Institute to inform you that after trying in vain for a long time to secure a suitable site for the Framji Cowasji Institute they have at last succeeded in contracting for the purchase of a spot which they consider a very eligible site in every respect for the Institute. You will observe from the accompanying plan of the premises I have forwarded for your inspection, that the spot in question colored red is situated at the South-West corner of the Framji Cowasji Tank, and a fine building erected on it will be seen from almost every point on

the Esplanade and its prominent situation appearing from a distance almost in a line with the two new buildings lately erected on the verge of the Esplanade by the Church Mission Society will greatly add to the beauty of the town when viewed from the Fort and whole of the Esplanade. On referring to the original title of the spot in question the Committee find that it is resumable by Government when required for public purposes by paying to the holder of it Rupees 2,500. The Committee therefore request you will be good enough to solicit Government on their behalf to give up their right of resuming the spot after it shall have been purchased for the Framji Cowasji Institute.

If you approve of this site and make over to the Committee the amount Government have been kind enough to promise to pay for purchasing a piece of ground for the Framji Cowasji Institute they will either purchase the buildings situated on the West of the site in question and enclosed within the pencil line drawn on the plan or obtain the permission of the Municipal Commissioners to allow the Committee to erect in the Tank 3 or 4 stone pillars marked in pencil 1. 2. 3. in the plan and to extend their proposed buildings over a portion of the Tank, to the pencil line marked A. B. in the plan, which concession, the Sub-Committee have every reason to believe, the Municipal Commissioners will have no objection to make, as this proposition, when carried out, will not only greatly add to the beauty of the Tank but also materially tend to the preservation of the water contained in it.

I have the honor to be,
Sir,
Your most obedient Servant,
NARAYEN DINANATHJI, Secretary.

BOMBAY, 8th September 1857.

No. 1897 of 1857.

BOMBAY OFFICE OF THE DIRECTOR OF

PUBLIC INSTRUCTION, 15*th December* 1857.

To

NARAYEN DiNANATHJI, ESQUIRE,

Secretary to the Framji Cowasji Institute.

SIR,

With reference to your letter dated 3rd September last, I have the honor to request that you will be kind enough to state for the information of the Right Honorable the Gvvernor in Council whether under present circumstances the fulfilment of the offer made by Government on behalf of the Framji Cowasji Institute, and which has been allowed to remain unavailable of so long, cannot be further postponed.

I have the honor to be,

Sir,

Your most obedient Servant,

E. I. HOWARD,

Director of Public Instruction.

To

E. I. HOWARD, ESQUIRE,

Director of Public Instruction.

SIR,

With reference to your lettter No. 1897 of 1857, dated 15th December 1857, I have been desired by the Sub-Committee of the Framji Cowasji Institute to state for the information of the Right Hon'ble the Governor in Council that under the circumstances alluded to in the letter under reply, that they cannot for a moment think of requesting his Lordship in Council to fulfil immediately the liberal offer, that has been made by Government. They are, however, glad to have it in their power to state, that one of their Committee who is a member of the family of the late Framji

Cowasji, Esq., has with a view to enable the Committee to commence with the building at once, offered to advance to them the amount promised to be paid by Government, on condition of Government repaying it to him, as soon as they can conveniently do so.

The Sub-Committee therefore trust that in the event of there being no other difficulty in the way, His Lordship in Council will be pleased to sanction the proposed arrangement, and permit the Sub-Committee to complete at once the purchase of the site they have selected for the building for they apprehend that in the event of their losing the opportunity of securing the site they have now in view they will meet with a very great difficulty in fixing upon another one so well suited for the purpose of the Institute, a difficulty that has up to this time prevented them from making any progress in the cause of the Institute.

I have the honor to be,

Sir,

Your most obedient Servant,

NARAYEN DINANATHJI, Secretary.

Bombay, 15th *January* 1858.

___

No. 298 of 1858.

General Department.

To

The DIRECTOR of PUBLIC INSTRUCTION.

The Civil Auditor.

Bombay Castle, 3rd *February* 1858.

Letter from the Director of Public Instruction, No. 124, dated the 16th January 1858.

Submits for the consideration of Government a request by the Committee of the Framji Cowasji Institute that, as Government desire to postpone the fulfilment of the offer made by them to contribute towards the purchase of a site for the Institute, they may be allowed to accept an offer made by a member of the family of the late Framji Cowasji, Esquire, to advance the sum promised by Government Rs. 12,000 on condition that it be repaid as soon as Government can conveniently do so.

Resolution of Government on the above, dated the 29th January 1858.

The Right Honorable the Governor in Council is pleased to accord his sanction to the arrangement proposed by the Sub-Committee of the Framji Cowasji Institution and recommended by the Director of Public Instruction.

2nd. As requested in paragraph 3rd of Mr. Howard's letter No. 1732, dated 28th October of 1857, Government undertake to give up their right of resuming the spot selected for the Institute as long as the ground be devoted *bonâ-fide* to the purposes for which the Institute is to be founded.

3. The necessary intimation should be made to the Revenue Department of the sanction accorded in paragraph 2.

(True Copy)

W. HART, Secretary to Government.

(True Copy)

E. I. HOWARD,
Director of Public Instruction.

128

No. 341 of 1858.

GENERAL DEPARTMENT.

To

THE DIRECTOR OF PUBLIC INSTRUCTION.

SIR,

I am directed to remind you that Government approve of the recommendation made by you in your letter No. 124, dated 16th January 1858, and alluded to at the close of paragraph 1 of Government Resolution No. 298, dated 3rd February 1858, involves the adoption of your suggestion that interest is not to be paid by Government on the amount to be advanced by a member of the late Framji Cowasji's Institute, and to request that the person who advances the money may be made to fully understand this (should he not do so already) before he pays it.

I have the honor to be,

Sir,

Your most obedient Servant,

W. HART, Secretary to Government.

(True Copy)

E. I. HOWARD,

Director of Public Instruction.

BOMBAY CASTLE, 8th *February* 1858.

BOMBAY, 25th *October* 1858.

E. I. HOWARD, ESQ.,

Director of Public Instruction, Bombay.

SIR,

I have been directed by the Committee of the Framji Cowasji Institute to state for the information of the Right Honorable the Governor in Council, that when they applied for the sanction of Government for the erection of a buildign

for the " Framji Cowasji Institute " on the site of the Alma
Hotel, at the South-West corner of the Framji Cowasji
Tank, they intended to apply to the Municipal Commissioners
for the use of the bullock shed at the south side of the
Tank, in order that the view of the proposed building may
not be obstructed by any high building between it and the
Girgaum road, and accordingly when they wrote to the
Commissioners for permission to extend the proposed building of the Framji Cowasji Institute over a portion of the
Tank, they requested that a portion of the bullock shed may
be transferred to the Institution, and that permission may
be granted for the construction of an open terrace on the
top of the remaining portion of it.

The Municipal Commissioners however while granting
their permission to the Committee for the extension of the
Framji Cowasji building over a portion of the Tank, intimated to them that the decision of the Commissioners with
regard to the bullock shed would be communicated to them
hereafter ; and they have since informed the Committee
that, as they have made over the bullock shed to Government for the use of the Native Dispensary, they are unable
to comply with the request of the Committee regarding the
bullock shed.

The Committee anticipating no difficulty in obtaining the
bullock shed, or at least a portion of it, have not only pull-
ed down the Alma Hotel (which cost them Rs. 5,500) for
preparing the land thereof for the intended Institute, but
have erected a wall in the Tank and are about to fill it up,
at an expense in all of about 2,000 Rupees. The Committee have now to their great disappointment been given
to understand that Government intend to construct one or
two stories on the top of the bullock shed, for the accommodation of the Native Dispensary, which it is proposed to

remove from its present locality ; and as by its doing so
the view of the proposed building for the Framji Cowasji
Institute, from the Girgaum road will not only be greatly
obstructed but the front part of the Institute can hardly be
completed without taking in a portion of the bullock shed ;
they beg to make the following proposal for the favorable
consideration of Government with an earnest hope that it
may meet with his Lordship's approbation.

That the bullock shed be made over to the Committee
entirely for the use of the Framji Cowasji Institute, on
condition of their providing for the use of the Native Dispensary a piece of ground out of the same Tank of the
same area as that occupied by the bullock shed, at the
North East corner of the Framji Cowasji Tank, by arching
over or filling up at their own expense a portion of the
Tank at that corner.

As the adoption of this proposal by Government would not
only prevent the interference of the two institutions with
one another, but also secure very eligible sites for both,
without subjecting either of them to any considerable additional expense. The Committee most respectfully request,
that you will do them the favour of submitting the proposal
for the favorable consideration of Government, and of obtaining their sanction to the same, otherwise they will be under
the necessity of giving up the idea of constructing on the
present site the proposed building for an Institute, which has
so long remained in abeyance for want of means and an
eligible site.

I have the honor to be,

Sir

Your most obedient Servant,

NARAYEN DINANATHJI,

Secretary to the Framji Cowasji Institute

No. 1561 of 1858.

PUBLIC WORKS DEPARTMENT,
CIVIL ARCHITECT'S OFFICE,
BOMBAY, 4th November 1858.

With reference to his letter dated 25th October 1858, to the Address of the Director of Public Instruction, the Secretary to the Committee of the Framji Cowasji Institute is requested to lend the undersigned the plans of the New Institute for inspection.

CHARLES FREDERICK NORTH, Major,
Civil Architect at the Bombay Presidency.

BOMBAY, 8th November 1858.

With reference to the Civil Architect's Memo. No. 1561 of 1858, dated the 4th November 1858, the undersigned begs to send him the accompanying plans of the proposed Institute for his inspection, and shall be happy to see him at any time that may suit his convenience for any explanation he may require on the subject.

NARAYEN DINANATHJI,
Secretary to the Framji Cowasji Institute.

(Copies)

No. 189 of 1858.

GOVERNMENT CENTRAL MUSEUM,
TOWN HALL, November 23rd, 1858.

To
THE SECRETARY TO GOVERNMENT,
GENERAL DEPARTMENT.

SIR,

In continuation of the subject of the latter portion of my letter No. 175, dated November 4th, 1858, to your address, I have the honor to inform you, that having first ascertained by personal visits (chiefly in company with Mr. Bhow Dajee, G.G.M.C.) to the leading members of the various Native communities of the Island, the unanimity of their desires to found an Economic Museum, and Natural History Gardens, on a scale worthy of Bombay, and finding that the great majority of them wish to connect the Establishment of such Institutions, with an expression of their affection for the Queen, I on the 18th instant issued printed invitations to 150 Native Gentlemen of mark to meet me here this afternoon to take into consideration the best means of carrying out their double project.

2. I believed it would be best furthered by means of a public meeting and on the gentlemen assembling at the appointed hour, I laid before them a requisition on the Sheriff of the Town which after an intelligent discussion was unanimously adopted. Its terms are as follows :—

To

    E. HEYCOCK, Esq.,

        Sheriff of Bombay.

SIR,

We the undersigned desirous of establishing some enduring testimony of the loyal devotion of the inhabitants of this Island to Her Most Gracious Majesty the Queen, request that you will be so good as to call as early as practicable a public meeting of the people of Bombay for the purpose of erecting an Economic Museum with Natural History and pleasure Gardens, to be styled in our sovereign's honor the Victoria Museum and Gardens.

                    We, &c.''

On Friday it will be forwarded to the Sheriff whom I shall beg to name an early day for the demonstration.

3. I first intend obtaining European signatures, for now that the value of the movement as having spontaneously originated on the part of the natives, has been realised, I think it desirable that the former should show their concurrence in it. The number and wealth however of the Native Communities are so greatly superior to that of the English located here, that with the former will necessarily rest the merit of almost wholly executing, as that of first conceiving the felicitous design.

4. When once the contemplated Institutions are seen established in Bombay, I believe that its example will be followed by all the leading towns of the Presidency each one of them will have its Victoria Museum and Gardens founded not by the Government but by the free desire and efforts of their inhabitants. I belive that the benefits that will result to the material interests of the country though incalculably great, are among the least that will flow from such sources. Their chiefest effect will be to draw together in harmonious intimacy Europeans and Natives, having with each other, without constraint day after day, in such places the most beneficial feelings of natural good-will and esteem must be engendered and perpetuated between them. I argue most happily from the realization of the schemes now under consideration, and I trust that when the public have subscribed the amount I expect from them, that it may be yet further swollen by help from the Horticultural Society. I intend officially applying to the trustees of the Framji Cowasji Institute to throw their means into the common fund, on the condition of carrying out the intentions of the endower of that Institute as regards preserving its individuality.

I have the honor to be,

Sir,

Your most obedient Servant,

GEORGE BIRDWOOD,

Secretary and Curator of the

Government Central Museum.

No. 3009 of 1858.

To

THE SECRETARY AND CURATOR OF THE
GOVERNMENT CENTRAL MUSEUM.

SIR,

I am directed to acknowledge the receipt of your letter
No. 189, dated 23rd November 1858, and in reply to inform
you that the project of the " Victoria Museum and Gardens "
is one which the Right Honorable the Governor in Council
cannot but approve of believing that it is calculated not
merely to develop production and natural wealth of the
country, but also to create a taste for observation and for
the study of many useful branches of knowledge, and that
those who are not benefitted by such an Institution may
derive amusement and gratification of a better an more intellectual kind than any that is now open to them.

2. But His Lordship in Council while desirous to encourage and promote this object does not lose sight of the recent
orders of the Honorable Court of Directors (of which a copy
is annexed) relative to the part to be taken by Government
in the carrying out of any object to which it is seen to
attach importance and towards which contributions from
the Public may be received, and his Lordship in Council
would therefore point out to you the necessity of avoiding
any proceedings which can possibly be misconstrued into an
undue exercise of the influence of Government in producing
subscriptions for the proposed Institution.

3. If the contributions of the wealthy Natives of Bombay to so excellent an object are clearly and unmistakeably
spontaneous the Governor in Council is confident that Her
Majesty's Government and the Council of India will rejoice
to find that so much public spirit, enlightenment and
loyalty exist among them.

4. The association of the Horticultural Society's Gardens with the proposed Museum has always appeared to his Lordship in Council most desirable, and he earnestly hopes that it will be found practicable.

5. If the Trustees of the Framji Cowasji Institute should connect that Institution with the proposed Victoria Museum, care will of course be taken to perpetuate the name and intentions of its benevolent founder.

I have the honor to be,

Sir,

Your most obedient Servant,

H. YOUNG, Chief Secretary.

(True Copies.)

N. D. CHAVES, Examiner.

To accompany Government letter, General Department, No. 3011, dated the 8th December 1858.

I have the honor to be,

Sir,

Your most obedient Servant,

H. YOUNG, Chief Secretary.

BOMBAY CASTLE, *8th December* 1858.

No. 19 OF 1858.

BOMBAY OFFICE of the DIRECTOR of

PUBLIC INSTRUCTION, *5th January* 1859.

To

NARAYEN DINANATHJI, Esq.,

Secretary to the Committee of the

Framji Cawasji Institute.

SIR,

With reference to your letter dated 25th October last, I have the honor to forward the accompanying copy of a Government letter No. 10 of the 4th instant, and the plan

alluded to therein, and to request that the Committee will
be kind enough to state for the information of Government
whether they are willing to take the Bullock shed on the
terms proposed by Government in paragraphs 2 and 3.

2. I beg at the same time to draw the attention of the
Committee to para. 3 of the Government letter.

I have the honor to be,
Sir,
Your most obedient Servant,

W. H. NEUNHAM,
For Director of Public Instruction.

No. 10 of 1859.

To

The DIRECTOR of PUBLIC INSTRUCTION.

Sir,

I am directed by the Right Honorable the Governor in
Council to acknowledge the receipt
Public Works Depart-
ment General Charit-
able Institutions.
of your letter, No. 2256, dated 27th
October 1858, with accompaniment,
and in reply to request that you will be good enough
to inform the Committee of the Framji Cowasji Institute with reference to the proposal made in their
Secretary's letter, dated 25th October 1858, to provide a
site for the Bombay Native Dispensary by filling in or
arching over on the North side of the Framji Cowasji Tank
an area equal to that occupied by the portico on the South
side of it on condition that the latter building be made over
to them, that the area offered would be insufficient for the
requirements of the Dispensary.

2. I am instructed also to request that you will desire
the Committee to state whether (supposing the consent of
the Municipal Commissioners and Mr. Ramlall Thacoor-

secdass be obtained) they would be willing to fill in or arch over the site indicated in the accompanying plan (showing the probable area and arrangements of the Dispensary, if erected on the North side of the Tank) receiving the Bullock shed in exchange.

3. In connection with this subject the attention of the Committee of the Framji Cowasji Institute should be drawn to the proposal contained in the correspondence forwarded to them with Government letter No. 3011, dated 8th December 1858, relative to the combination or union of the Institute with the proposed " Victoria Museum and Gardens." This arrangement if approved and adopted, would necessitate a reconsideration of the whole matter.

I have the honor to be,

Sir,

Your most obedient Servant,

H. YOUNG, Chief Secretary.

(True Copy.)

W. H. NEUNHAM,

For Director of Public Instruction.

Bombay Castle, *4th January* 1859.

To

JUGGANNATH SUNKERSET, Esq.

NARAYEN DINANATHJI, Esq.

Gentlemen,

I am directed by the Committee of the Bombay Native Dispensary to transmit to you the annexed copy of a letter from Captain W. F. Marriott, dated 11th January 1859, on behalf of the Committee of the New Sailors' Home, to the address of the Collector of Bombay, relative to a suitable house being provided for the Dispensary for temporary occupation to enable the Sailors' Home Committee to commence without further delay the erection of the New Sailors' Home on the site on which the buildings at present occupied by the Dispensary stand, and to request that you will be good enough to meet Captain Marriott and Mr. F. Hutchinson on the subject of Captain Marriott's letter and to report the result of your conference to the Committee.

I have the honor to be,

Gentlemen,

Your most obedient Servant,

JAMES H. VITTERS,

Acting Secretary.

BOMBAY, 11*th January* 1859.

To

F. HUTCHINSON, Esq ,

Collector, &c.

MY DEAR MR. HUTCHINSON,

Government, in stating to the Committee for the new Sailors' Home the difficulties and probable delays in providing a new site for the Dispensary, have added that " if the Committee of the Sailors' Home will in meanwhile provide a house suitable for the Dispensary for temporary occupation, Government will have no objection to its removal from the buildings occupied by it and the immediate surrender of the same to the Committee of the Sailors' Home."

On behalf of the Committee, I write to ask your kind assistance in procuring a suitable House. If the arrangement regarding " Cardiff Castle" which you suggested could be carried out, the Committee would be very glad, and if it be in your power to ascertain both the consent of the Committee of the Dispensary and of the owners of the house, the Sailors' Home Committee would be exceedingly obliged by your concluding the arrangement for them.

Possibly I am asking more than you can conveniently do, but if you could kindly undertake the arrangement, the Committee hereby authorize and confirm such agreement as you may make on their behalf.

Of course the terms should provide the power of giving up the house without a very long notice.

Believe me, yours faithfully,

W. FRED. MARRIOTT,

on behalf of the Committee.

(True Copy.)

JAMES H. VITTERS, Acting Secretary,

Bombay Native Dispensary.

To

EDWARD HOWARD, Esq.,

Director of Public Instruction, Bombay.

Sir,

With reference to your letter No. 19, dated the 5th of January last, I have the honor at the desire of the Committee of the Framji Cowasji Institute to state for the information of the Right Honorable the Governor in Council that they are unable to accept the offer of Government on the terms proposed in paragraphs 2 and 3 of Mr. Chief Secretary Young's letter No. 10 of the 4th January 1859 to your address, the Funds at the disposal of the Committee not permitting them to do so.

Adverting to the 3rd paragraph of the Government letter, the Committee have instructed me to state for the information of His Lordship in Council that they do not intend to unite the Framji Cowasji Institute with the Victoria Museum and Gardens. Should Government however resolve to make over the Bullock shed to the Native Dispensary, the Committee apprehend that the spot of ground on which it is proposed to erect a building for the Framji Cowasji Institute, would be rendered quite unsuitable for that purpose, and they have therefore no alternative but to offer that Spot of Ground to the Government at its cost price if required for their use.

In the event of Government not requiring the ground the Committee request that they may be permitted to sell it to any private individual that may be desirous of purchasing it from them, and be allowed to enclose and fill up with the consent of the Municipal Commissioners a portion of the Framji Cowasji Tank, at its nothern side sufficient for the erection of the proposed building for the Framji Cowasji Institute.

The plans which accompanied the Government letter to your address No. 10 of 1859 are herewith returned.

I have the honor to be,

Sir,

Your most obedient Servant,

NARAYEN DINANATHJI, Secretary.

BOMBAY, *9th May* 1859.

No. 1978 OF 1859.

POONA OFFICE OF THE DIRECTOR OF
PUBLIC INSTRUCTION, 15*th September* 1859.

To

NARAYEN DINANATHJI, ESQUIRE,

Secretary to the Framji Cowasji Institute.

SIR,

With reference to your letter dated 9th May last, I have the honor to forward the annexed copy of a letter from Government No. 2380, dated 14th Instant, and to request that you will have the goodness to report the actual cost of the ground for the information of Government at your earliest convenience.

I have the honor to be,

Sir,

Your most obedient Servant,

E. I. HOWARD, Director of Public Instruction.

No. 2380 of 1859.

To

THE DIRECTOR of PUBLIC INSTRUCTION.

SIR,

I am directed by the Right Honorable the Governor in

Public Works Department General Charitable Institutions.

Council to acknowledge the receipt of your letter No. 1614, dated 4th August 1859, and in reply to inform you that Government are disposed to accept of the offer of the Committee of the Framji Cowasji Institute to sell at cost price the spot of ground on which it was proposed to erect a building for the Institute, but I am to request in the first instance that you will be good enough to ascertain and report the actual cost of the ground.

I have the honor to be,

Sir,

Your most obedient Servant,

H. YOUNG, Chief Secretary.

(True Copy.)

EDWARD I. HOWARD,

Director of Public Instruction.

BOMBAY CASTLE, 14*th September* 1859.

To

EDWARD I. HOWARD, ESQUIRE,

Director of Public Instruction.

SIR,

With reference to your letter No. 1978 of 1859, dated the 15th September 1859, I have been instructed by the Committee of the Framji Cowasji Institute to request that as the Bullock shed is no longer required for the use of the Native Dispensary the Right Honorable the Governor in Council will do them the favour to make over the shed to them on their paying a sum of Rs. 2,000 as a contribution towards recovering from the Tank a suitable piece of ground for the Native Dispensary.

The Committee have been given to understand that this arrangement will be agreed to by the Committee of the Native Dispensary and they therefore hope that there will be no objection on the part of his Lordship in Council to comply with their request.

I have the honor to be,

Sir,

Your most obedient Servant,

NARAYEN DINANATHJI,

Secretary to the Framji Cowasji Institute.

BOMBAY, 16th December 1859.

To

E. I. HOWARD, ESQUIRE,

Director of Public Instruction,

Poona.

SIR,

With reference to your letter of the 21st ultimo, I have been directed by the Managing Committee of the Framji Cawasji Institute to inform you that the present site of the proposed Institute has already cost the Committee a sum of Rs. 6,514 besides interest to the amount of about Rs. 800.

I have the honor to be,

Sir,

Your most obedient Servant,

NARAYEN DINANATHJI, Secretary.

4th January 1860.

No. 291 of 1860.

MEMORANDUM.

The undersigned requests that the Secretary to the Committee of the Framji Cowasji Institute will have the goodness to state what is the area of the plot purchased and of that reclaimed from the Framji Cowasji Tank, as a building site for the Framji Cowasji Institute, and what is the present condition of the site.

H. YOUNG,
Chief Secretary to Government.

Bombay Castle, 3rd February 1860.

To

HENRY YOUNG, Esquire,
Chief Secretary to Government,
Bombay.

Sir,

In acknowledging the receipt of your Memo. No. 291 of the 3rd instant, I have the honor the state for the information of the Right Honorable the Governor in Council that the area of the plot purchased is about 560 square yards, and that of the ground reclaimed from the Framji Cowasji Tank about 361 square yards, amounting altogether to about 921 square yards, the old house that has stood on the plot purchased, having been removed, the whole site is now in a condition fit for erecting a building thereon.

I have the honor to be,
Sir,
Your most obedient Servant,
NARAYEN DINANATHJI,
Secretary to the Framji Cowasji Institute.

Bombay, 9th February 1860.

No. 567 of 1860.

PUBLIC WORKS DEPARTMENT,
GENERAL SCIENTIFIC INSTITUTIONS,
BOMBAY CASTLE, 13th March 1860.

To

THE DIRECTOR OF PUBLIC INSTRUCTION,
THE ACTING COLLECTOR OF BOMBAY,
THE ACCOUNTANT GENERAL,
THE CIVIL AUDITOR,
THE GENERAL PAYMASTER.

Letter from the Director of Public Instructon, No. 107, dated the 17th January 1860.

With reference to Government letter No. 2380 of the 14th September 1859, forwards copy of a letter from the Secretary to the Committee of the Framji Cowasji Institute, stating that the present site of the proposed Institute has already cost the Committee a sum of Rs. 6,514 besides interest to the amount of about Rs. 800.

Letter from the Secretary to the Committee of the Framji Cowasji Institute, dated 9th February 1860.

States the area of the site and describes its present condition.

RESOLUTION OF GOVERNMENT on the above, dated the 29th February 1860.

His Lordship in Council resolves that as the price of the ground tendered to Government is moderate (about Rs. 7 per square yard) considering the position it occupies it should be purchased on account of Government, although the question as to whether the museum will or will not be permitted to be erected on the present site of the Marine line is still undecided.

(True Copy.)
H. YOUNG, Chief Secretary.

To
EDWARD HOWARD, Esquire,
Director of Public Instruction, Bombay.
Sir,

With reference to your Memo. No. 550 of 1860, dated the 15th March last, forwarding to me copy of Government Resolution dated the 19th of February 1860, to the effect that the ground tendered to Government by the Committee of the Framji Cowasji Institute should be purchased by Government, I have been instructed by the Committee to bring to the notice of the Right Honorable the Governor in Council the peculiar circumstances under which the Committee tendered the ground to Government. That it was when they saw that Government was determined to grant the Bullock shed for the use of the Native Dispensary that they were obliged to make the offer with certain conditions as will appear from the following extract of a letter dated the 9th May 1859.

" Should Government, however, resolve to make over the Bullock shed to the Native Dispensary, the Committee apprehend that the spot of ground on which it is proposed to erect a building for the Framji Cowasji Institute would be rendered quite unsuitable for that purpose, and they have therefore no alternative but to offer that spot of ground to Government at its cost price if required for their use."

" In the event of Government not requiring the ground the Committee request that they may be permitted to sell to any private individual that may be desirous of purchasing it from them, and be allowed to enclose and fill up with the consent of the Municipal Commissioners a portion of the Framji Cowasji Tank at its Northern side sufficient for the erection of the proposed building for the Framji Cowasji Institute."

As soon, however, as the Committee were given to understand that the Bullock shed was not suited for the purpose of the Native Dispensary, and that the Government was no longer desirous of making it over to that Institution, they immediately forwarded to you on the 16th December 1859 the following letter, and they are very sorry to see that Government has not taken into its consideration the request contained therein when passing their Resolution of the 29th February last.

" With reference to your letter No. 1978 of 1859, dated the 15th September 1859, I have been instructed by the Committee of the Framji Cowasji Institute to request that as the Bullock shed is no longer required for the use of the Native Dispensary the Right Honorable the Governor in Council will do them the favour to make over the shed to them on their paying Rs. 2,000 as a contribution towards recovering from the Tank a suitable piece of ground for the Native Dispensary."

" The Committee have been given to understand that this arrangement will be agreed to by the Committee of the Native Dispensary, and they therefore hope that there will be no objection on the part of His Lordship in Council to comply with their request." Dated 16th December 1859.

It will therefore clearly appear from the above communications that when the offer of the ground was made to Government the Committee firmly believed that Government was determined to make over the bullock shed to the Native Dispensary."

The offer therefore was made not from any desire on the part of the Committee to get rid of the site—but solely with the view of not coming in the way of Government granting the bullock shed to the Native Dispensary and as Government no longer intends to make over the shed to that institution the Committee beg that the Right Honorable the Governor in Council will be pleased to take into favorable consideration their request contained in their letter of the 16th December 1859.

I have the honor to be,
Sir,
Your most obedient Servant,
NARAYEN DINANATHJI, Secretary.
Bombay, 5th May 1860.

No. 345 of 1860.

Public Works Department,
Executive Engineer's Office, P.D.
Poona, 27th April 1860.

To
Mr. ARDASIR FRAMJI,
Secretary to the Framji Cowasji Institute.

Sir,

Having learnt that Government have invited the Framji Cowasji Institute Committee to add their funds to the Victoria Museum on condition of being provided with separate accommodation under the same roof, and having been appointed by Government to prepare designs for the Victoria Museum and a number of other public buildings proposed to be erected on the esplanade, I have the honor to request you will lay the letter before the Committee and favor me with any information tending to the object in view. I particularly desire to be informed of the amount and nature of the accommodation that would be required by the Institute, and also of the amount which the Committee would be prepared to pay for the accommodation so furnished them, in what, it is to be hoped will prove one of the Finest Edifices in Bombay.

I have the honor to be,
Sir,
Your most obedient Servant,
H. S. T. WILKINS, Captain,
Executive Engineer on Special Duty, P.D.

To

CAPTAIN H. S. T. WILKINS,

Executive Engineer on Special Duty, Bombay.

SIR,

With reference to your letters No. 345 of the 17th ultimo and No. 391 of the 10th instant, to the address of Mr. Ardasir Framji, on the subject of the Framji Cowasji Institute, I have the honor to forward to you the accompanying extract from a letter addressed to Government by the Secretary to the Committee of the Framji Cowasji Institute under date the 9th May 1859, on the subject in question, by which you will perceive that no arrangement has been come to with Government as regards the proposed amalgamation.

Under these circumstances, the Committee is not, I am instructed to state, in a position to make any arrangement with you in this matter.

I have the honor to be,

Sir,

Your most obedient Servant,

S. P. FRAMJI,

On behalf of the Secretary,

NARAYEN DINANATHJI.

BOMBAY, 1st May 1860.

EXTRACT from a letter dated 9th May 1859, addressed to Government by the Secretary to the Committee of the Framji Cowasji Institute.

" Adverting to the 3rd paragraph of the Government letter, the Committee have instructed me to state for the information of His Lordship in Council that they do not intend to unite the Framji Cowasji Institute with the Victoria Museum and Gardens."

(A True Extract.)

S. P. FRAMJI.

To

Dr. BHAWOO DAJEE

AND

Dr. BIRDWOOD,

Secretaries to the Victoria Museum
Committee, Bombay.

GENTLEMEN,

I have been instructed by the Managing Committee of the Framji Cowasji Institute to communicate to you for the information of the Victoria Museum Committee, their opinion that it would greatly add to the advantage of the Institute, were the Victoria Museum built close to, and if possible, in one harmonious plan, with the Framji Cowasji Institute.

I have also been instructed by them to submit the following proposals for the favourable consideration of the Victoria Museum Committee.

That the Framji Cowasji Institute making over to the Victoria Museum Committee, the philosophical apparatus and the collection of minerals, &c., of the value of about six or seven thousand Rupees, and further to the Museum Committee such a sum of money as would make up, with the value of the above mentioned apparatus, minerals, &c., a sum equal to Rupees ten thousand. That in consideration of the above the Victoria Museum Committee appropriate a gallery, in the proposed Victoria Museum building, to the formation of a Natural History Museum, to be called after the name of the late Framji Cowasji and to be under the management of the Committee of the Framji Cowasji Institute, or the Students' Literary and Scientific Society.

I have the honor to be,
Gentlemen,
Your most obedient Servant,
NARAYEN DINANATHJI.

BOMBAY, 17th September, 1861.

To

E. I. HOWARD, Esquire,
Director of Public Instruction.

SIR,

I have been instructed by the Committee of the Framji Cowasji Institute to write to you for the information of the Right Honorable the Governor in Council, that they have at last resolved to erect the proposed building for the Framji Cowasji Institute, on the site of the Alma Hotel and the ground reclaimed by them from the Framji Cowasji Tank.

I have also been instructed by them to request that the Right Honorable the Governor in Council will early favor them with a compliance of the request contained in their letter to your address, dated the 16th of May 1860.

I have the honor to be,

Sir,

Your most obedient Servant,

NARAYEN DINANATHJI,

Secretary.

BOMBAY, 18*th September* 1861.

CHAPTER XV.

Correspondence with the Board of Commissioners.

To

The MUNICIPAL COMMISSIONERS
FOR THE ISLAND OF BOMBAY.

GENTLEMEN,

I have been desired by the Sub-Committee of the Framji Cowasji Institute to write to you that they have all along been very desirous of erecting a building for the above named Institution near the Framji Cowasji Tank with a view that the works which bear the name of that much respected Gentleman and which are intended wholly for the benefit of the public at large, may be grouped together in one locality that after a great many fruitless attempts to attain this subject which unfortunately extended over a very long period, they have at last succeeded in securing a suitable site by purchasing the premises called the Alma Hotel situate at the South-West corner of the Framji Cowasji Tank and marked A in the accompanying plan of the premises. The piece of ground thus secured is not however large enough for the building intended to be erected on it and the Sub-Committee therefore request that you will do them the favor of permitting them to construct stone pillars in the Tank at its South-West corner on the lines marked B C and C D in the plan, to extend the proposed building to these lines which will be about 10 feet from the present wall of the Tank, to make over to them the paved passage between the Alma Hotel premises and wall of the Tank and the bullock shed, also a very small portion of the shed as far as the point where the line mark B C of the intended stone pillars in the Tank would if produced towards the South meet the line formed by the exteriors or southern row of pillars of the bullock-shed.

I have been further desired by the Sub-Committee to request your permission to convert the roof of the bullock-

shed into an elegantly railed terrace under the superintendence of the Superintendent of Repairs and according to
the design furnished to them by that officer and approved
by you leaving the lower part under the roof untouched and
to open a communication from the proposed terrace to the
Framji Cowasji Institute in order that the public who may
resort to the Institute to hear lectures or for any other
purpose may have an opportunity of enjoying the benefit of
the open air on the terrace.

The Sub-Committee in preferring this request on behalf
of the Institute hope that as the Framji Cowasji Institute
will be a very useful and important Institution to the public
at large, that as a very large sum of money was expended
on the enlargement and improvement of the Framji Cowasji
Tank by that respected Parsee Gentleman in commemoration of whom the Institute has been established, that as the
whole of the Ground along the South-West corner of the
Tank as well as that portion of the Tank itself over which
the Sub-Committee are desirous of extending the proposed
building was, the Sub-Committee have been given to understand purchased by the late Framji Cowasji, Esquire, and
made over for the use and benefit of the public, that as the
compliance by you with the request of the Sub-Committee
will in no way cause any inconvenience to the public or
injury to the Framji Cawasji Tank or to the adjacent
bullock shed—the latter of which will soon become
quite useless for any Municipal purpose whatsoever
as soon as the Vehar water-works shall have been
completed,—but on the contrary tend greatly to improve
the general appearance, and that as the proposed
Framji Cowasji Institute grouped together with the two
magnificent buildings erected by the Mission Society
on the verge of the esplanade will generally improve the
appearance of the Native Town when viewed from the foot
or along the road leading from it to the town, the request
of the Sub-Committee contained in this letter will be complied with by you and to represent that your compliance

will confer a very great boon on the whole community of Bombay for whose benefit the Framji Cowasji Institute has been established.

I have the honor to be,

Gentlemen,

Your most obedient Servant,

NARAYEN DINANATHJI, Secretary.

BOMBAY, 3rd March 1858.

No. 1124 OF 1858.

To

NARAYEN DINANATHJI, ESQUIRE,

Secretary to the Framji Cowasji Institute.

SIR,

I have the honor by direction of the Municipal Commissioners, to acknowledge the receipt of your letter bearing date the 3rd instant, and in reply to inform you that the Commissioners have no objection to the construction of the proposed building for the Framji Cowasji Institution or to the arching over of part of the Tank, as shown in the Plan forwarded with your letter.

As regards your request that a portion of the Bullock shed may be made over to the Institution, and that permission may be given for the construction of a terrace over the remaining portion of the shed, I am desired to observe that the decision of the Commissioners will be communicated to you hereafter.

The plan which accompanied your letter is herewith returned.

I have the honor to be,

Sir,

Your most obedient Servant,

F. HUTCHINSON,

Clerk to the Board of Commissioners.

MUNICIPAL COMMISSIONER'S OFFICE,

BOMBAY 19th March 1858.

To

F. HUTCHINSON, Esquire,

        Clerk to the Municipal Commissioners, Bombay.

Sir,

On the receipt of your letter conveying to the Committee of the Framji Cowasji Institute permission of the Municipal Commissioners to construct a series of stone pillars in the Framji Cowasji Tank at its South West corner in a line parallel to the Southern portion of the Western parapet wall as indicated in their first letter to the Commissioners the Committee proceeded to take the requisite measures for erecting the stone pillars when to their disappointment found that the parapet as well as the foundation wall, in question was not erect but was inclined full 6 inches towards the tank and was consequently not strong enough in the opinion of the professional gentleman to sustain the weight of the two storied massive building proposed to be erected on that spot for the Framji Cowasji Institute and the course he suggested to overcome this difficulty was to construct a solid wall in the tank along the line of the proposed pillars and to have the space between it and present wall opposite to it filled up.

This would take away a small portion of the tank but would not in their opinion much curtail the usefuluess of the tank as the part proposed to be filled up is almost dry at the close of the dry season when water is most wanted and it is situated at the Western side of the tank from which the water can never come into the tank but through which it always finds its way to the sea. Besides the supply of water in the tank cannot possibly be of any great use to the people except for the ensuing year by which the Island of Bombay is almost sure to be supplied with waters from the Vehar water works. The only part of the Tank on which the supply of water at the close of the dry season can depend, is at its Southern side where moats are at work,

where the water is deepest, and where it is now being drawn
from and the Committee engage in the event of the Municipal Commissioners permitting them to fill up the portion
of the tank, to excavate and deepen at their own charge
that portion of it which is immediately under the moats,
should the supply of water in the tank fail at any period of
the next dry season.

The Committee therefore hope that under the circumstances represented above the Municipal Commissioners will
be pleased to permit them to fill up the portion of the tank
above indicated them.

I have the honor to be,

Sir,

Your most obedient Servant,

NARAYEN DINANATHJI, Secretary.

BOMBAY, *9th June* 1858.

No. 2198 OF 1858.

To

NARAYEN DINANATHJI, ESQUIRE,

Secretary to the Framji Cowasji Institute.

SIR,

I have the honor, by desire of the Municipal Commissioners, to acknowledge the receipt of your letter dated
the 9th instant, and, in reply, to inform you that, under the
circumstances represented, the Commissioners comply
with the request therein made.

I have the honor to be,

Sir,

Your most obedient Servant,

F. HUTCHINSON,

Clerk to the Board of Conservancy.

MUNICIPAL COMMISSIONER'S OFFICE,

BOMBAY, *15th June* 1858.

To

    H. AHER, ESQUIRE,

          Superintendent of Repairs, Bombay.

SIR,

I have the honor to forward herewith Copy of a plan showing the line of the proposed pillars or a wall to be erected in the Framji Cowasji Tank for the purpose of the Framji Cowasji Institute. The space on the West and North of the dotted lines marked A. B. and C. D. include the ground originally applied for and that required for the broad foundation of pillars and sloping of a wall in the event of its being sanctioned by the Municipal Commissioners instead of the permission already granted for the erection of pillars and have to request that you will be good enough to have the said line marked out in the tank so as to enable us to begin with the erection of stone pillars on the points B. C. and D. immediately.

        I have the honor to be,

              Sir,

        Your most obedient Servant,

          NARAYEN DINANATHJI, Secretary.

BOMBAY, 15th June 1858.

To

              No. 2227 OF 1858.

    NARAYEN DINANATHJI, ESQUIRE,

          Secretary to the Framji Cawasji Institute.

SIR,

I have the honor to inform you that the Municipal Commissioners have no objection to your constructing the proposed walls, in the Framji Cowasji Tank on the site shown on the Plan which accompanied your letter of the 15th inst.

        I have the honor to be,

              Sir,

        Your most obedient Servant,

          F. HUTCHINSON,

           Clerk to the Board of Conservancy.

MUNICIPAL COMMISSIONER'S OFFICE,

    BOMBAY, 18th June 1858.

No. 2247 of 1858.

To

NARAYEN DINANATHJI, Esquire,

Secretary to the Framji Cowasji Institute.

Sir,

With reference to the 2nd para. of my letter No. 1124, dated 19th March last, on the subject of your request that a portion of the Bullock shed, at the Framji Cowasji Tank, may be made over for the purpose of the proposed building for the Framji Cowasji Institution, I have the honor to inform you, by desire of the Municipal Commissioners, that, in consequence of an application from Government, they have connected to make over to them, on the Vehar water works coming into operation, the Bullock shed in question, in order that the site of it may be appropriated for a new building, for the Native Dispensary; and that they regret, therefore, that they are unable to comply with the request of your Committee to be permitted to construct a terrace over the Bullock shed, in connection with the building proposed to be erected for the Institute.

I have the honor to be,

Sir,

Your most obdient Servant,

F. HUTCHINSON,
Clerk to the Board of Conservancy.

Municipal Commissioner's Office,
Bombay, 21st June 1858.

CHAPTER XVI.

Miscellaneous Correspondence.

To
RUSTOMJI COWASJI BANAJI, Esq.,
Oalcutta.

Sir,

I have the honor to forward the accompanying copy of the proceedings of a meeting held in the Library of the Elphinstone Institution to commemorate the name of the late Framji Cowasji, Esquire, as it has been suggested that you might wish to unite with his friends in Bombay to do honor to the memory of one so much esteemed by all who knew him.

The proposed Institute has received the approbation of all the most influential natives of Bombay, and it is hoped, will be of great use in spreading a knowledge of the Arts and Sciences of Europe throughout this Presidency.

Should you approve of the proposal I would request your influence with such other friends of the deceased as you think likely to aid in the undertaking.

I am,
Your most obedient Servant,
JOSEPH PATTON, Secretary.

BOMBAY, 17*th October* 1851.

To
NUSSERVANJI BOMANJI MODEE
AND
COWASJI SHAPOORJI LUNGDANA,
Canton.

Gentlemen,

I have the honor to forward the accompanying copy of the proceedings of a meeting held in the Library of the Elphinstone Institution to commemorate the name of the late Framji Cowasji, Esquire, as it has been suggested that you might wish to unite in showing your respect for the memory of one so much esteemed by all who knew him.

The proposed Institute has received the approval of all the most influential gentlemen of Bombay, and, if carried into effect, will have great influence in raising the character of the people of this Presidency. Should you approve of the proposal, I would request your influence with such other friends of the deceased as would be likely to aid the undertaking.

I remain,
Gentlemen,
Your most obedient Servant,
JOSEPH PATTON, Secretary.
Bombay, 18th November 1851.

To
JOSEPH PATTON, Esq.,
Professor Elphinstone Institution, Bombay.
Sir,

I have the honor to acknowledge the receipt of your letter of the 7th instant, enclosing a copy of the proceedings of a meeting held in the Library of the above Institution for the purpose of raising a fund from among the friends and acquaintances of my late lamented brother Framji Cowasji to be applied towards the formation of a museum of Arts and Sciences in commemoration of the memory of that worthy Individual. I quite approve of the proposal and beg to tender the Projectors of this laudable plan for perpetuating the memory of one so deserving, as well as to yourself my best thanks for not having forgotten me. I shall endeavour, all I can, to influence a subscription here among my friends and shall in due time communicate to you the result.

I remain,
Sir,
Your most obedient Servant,
RUSTOMJI COWASJI.
Calcutta, 29th October 1851.

CANTON, *28th December* 1851.

To

JOSEPH PATTON, Esquire.

DEAR SIR,

We take great pleasure in acknowledging the receipt of your esteemed favour with its enclosures which came to hand on the 16th instant per the " Ganges " stating the object of the Testimonial raised in Bombay to perpetuate the name of the late lamented Framji Cowasji, Esquire, and requesting us to join in the project.

Agreeably to your request we have exercised our best influence and weight where we knew it would be of any effect and are now glad to inform you that the greater portion of our Parsee community here have ably testified their respect for the above deceased gentleman by contributing to the aforesaid testimonial the sum of Dollars 225, which we beg to remit to you in Bill No. 61190 drawn by the Oriental Bank on the same Bank of your place for Rs. 528¾ at Rs. 235 per 100, we hope will be acceptable to your Committee. Herein we have much pleasure to enclose a copy of the list of the parties subscribing the above amount.

In conclusion we beg to offer our earnest thanks to you for permitting us to join our Bombay friends in commemorating the name of our late lamented fellow countrymen.

We have the honor to be,

Sir,

Your most obedient servants,

NUSSERWANJI BOMANJI MODEE AND
COWASJI SHAPOORJI LUNGDANA.

LIST OF SUBSCRIBERS RESIDENT IN CANTON TO FRAMJI COWASJI TESTIMONIAL.

	Dollars.
Dadabhoy Nusserwanji Mody and Co	31
Cowasji Shapoorji Lungdana	31
Pestonji Framji Cama and Co	25
Pestonji Dorabji Nusserwanji Camaji and Co	25
Cursetji Rustomji Camajee	25
Edulji Framji Sons and Co	15
Cowasji Pallunji and Co	10
Nusserwanji Ardaseer Bansa and Co	10
David Sassoon Sons and Co	10
Rustomji Byramji and Co	5
Byramji Cooverji Bhabha	5
Herjeebhoy Ardaseer and Co	5
Jehangeer Framji Buxey	5
Burjorji Sorabji	5
Hormusji Jamasji Nadershaw	2
Pestonji Jamsetji Motteewalla	2
Pallunji Nusserwanji Patell	2
Pestonji Byramji Colah	2
Aderji Shapoorji Goozratee	2
Cowasji Edulji Khumbata	3
Dossabhoy Hormusji Dolakhaw	1
Cursetji Rustomji Daver	2
Edulji Cursetji	2

Total dollars ... 225

NARAYEN DINANATHJI, Esquire,
Secretary to the Framji Cowasji
Institute Committee.

DEAR SIR,

As I am about to quit Bombay permanently, I beg you will do the favour to submit my resignation of the Chair to members of the Committee.

With my cordial wishes for the success of the Institution and thanks for the support I have received from the Members and yourself while I have occupied the Chair.

I beg to subscribe myself,
Yours most faithfully,

BOMBAY, 16th May 1853. J. M. LEGEYT.

STUDENTS' LITERARY AND SCIENTIFIC SOCIETY,
BOMBAY, 24th December 1853.

To

NARAYEN DINANATHJI, Esquire,
Secretary to the Framji Cowasji
Institute Committee.

SIR,

In accordance to a Resolution passed at a meeting of the Managing Committee of the Society, held on the 20th instant, I beg to make over to you by the enclosed Cheque of Rs. 3,112-1-6, on the Commercial Bank, the balance as in the margin, of the Framji Cowasji Apparatus Fund.

	Rs.	a.	p.
Department Receipt of Commercial Bank	2,577	9	2
Interest Receipt	227	7	10
Balance in Commercial Bank	307	0	6
Rs.	3,112	1	6

You will be pleased to pass me a receipt for the same.

I remain,
Sir,
Your most obedient Servant,
BOMANJI PESTONJI, Treasurer.

To

THE HONORABLE J. WARDEN, ESQUIRE.

SIR,

I have the honor to inform you that at a meeting of the Committee of the Framji Cowasji Institute, held in the rooms of the Elphinstone Institution on the 8th instant, it was resolved unanimously that you be requested to be Chairman of the Committee in the room of P. W. LeGeyt, Esq., resigned.

I therefore request you to do the Committee the favor of accepting the office.

I have the honor to be,
Sir,
Your most obedient Servant,
NARAYEN DINANATHJI, Secretary.

BOMBAY, 20th April 1854.

To

N ARAYEN DINANATHJI, ESQUIRE,

Secretary to the Framji Cowasji
Institute Committee.

SIR,

I have had the honor to receive your letter, dated yesterday, informing me that, at a meeting of the Managing Committee of the Framji Cowasji Institute, it was resolved unanimously that I be requested to be Chairman of the Committee.

I beg you to convey to the Committee the expression of my willingness to accept the office to which they have done me the honor to nominate me.

I have the honor to be,
Sir,
Your most obedient Servant,

BOMBAY, 21st April 1854.   JAMES WARDEN.

164

To

PROFESSOR GIRAUD,
PROFESSOR DADABHOY NOWROJI,
AND
ARDASEER FRAMJI, ESQUIRE.

GENTLEMEN,

I have been directed by the Committee of the Framji Cowasji Institute to communicate to you, that they shall feel much obliged by your forming yourself into a Committee to take charge of the philosophical apparatus, specimens of minerals, &c., belonging to the F. C. Institute, and at present deposited in the Elphinstone Institution.

I have the honor to be,
Gentlemen,
Your most obedient Servant,
NARAYEN DINANATHJI,
BOMBAY, 24th October 1854.   Secretary.

To

NARAYEN DINANATHJI, ESQUIRE,
Secretary to the Framji Cowasji Institute.

SIR,

Having been desired by the Head Master of the Elphinstone Central School, to remove the cases containing the collection of rocks and minerals belonging to the Framji Cowasji Institute, now lying at the school, I have rented a portion of the premises below the Native General Library, occupied by Mr. Sorabji Framji, for Rs. 7 per month, to place the cases from May 25th, 1858.

I remain,
Sir,
Your most obedient Servant,
ARDASEER FRAMJI,
BOMBAY, 7th July 1858.   Curator.

To

PROFESSOR HUGHLINGS,
Secretary to the Students' Literary and
Scientific Society, Bombay.

SIR,

I have been instructed by the Committee of the Framji Cowasji Institute to inform you, that they are of opinion that it would greatly add to the advantage of the Institute were the Victoria Museum built close to, and if possible, in one harmonious plan with it ; and that they have passed a Resolution making the following proposals to the Committee of the Victoria Museum.

That the Framji Cowasji Institute make over to the Victoria Museum Committee the philosophical apparatus, and the collection of minerals, &c., of the value of six or seven thousand Rupees, and that they pay to the Museum Committee such a further sum, as would make up, with the value of the abovementioned apparatus, minerals, &c., a sum equal to ten thousand rupees.

That in consideration of the above, the Victoria Museum appropriate a gallery in the proposed Victoria Museum building, to the formation of a natural History Museum, to be called after the name of the late Framji Cowasji, and to be under the management of the Framji Cowasji Institute, or the Students' Literary and Scientific Society.

I have further been instructed to inform you, that they have resolved to invite tenders at once for the erection of the proposed building for the Framji Cowasji Institute on the site of the Alma Hotel, and the ground reclaimed from the Framji Cowasji Tank.

I have the honor to be,
Sir,
Your most obedient Servant,
NARAYEN DINANATHJI,

BOMBAY, 18th September 1861.   Secretary.

To

ARDASIR FRAMJI, Esquire.

Sir,

I have the honor to inform you that the Committee of the Framji Cowasji Institute have resolved to make over to Dr. G. Birdwood for safe custody the philosophical apparatus, minerals, &c., now in your charge, and to request you will be good enough to inform me, when it will be convenient to you, to make over the same to that gentleman.

I have the honor to be,
Sir,
Your most obedient Servant,
NARAYEN DINANATHJI,

Bombay, 18th September 1861.   Secretary.

———

To

Sir ALEXANDER GRANT, Bart.

My dear Sir,

With reference to your note dated the 31st ultimo, I beg to inform you that the building of the Framji Cowasji Institute has not been commenced yet, but plans and specifications of the building have been prepared, and tenders have been invited and received. The arrangements for commencing the building will be completed as soon as a reply to a reference that has been made to Government is received and the building will probably be finished in about a year.

Believe me,
Dear Sir,
Yours sincerely,
JUGGUNNATH SUNKERSETT.

Bombay, 4th October 1861.

To

JUGGUNNATH SUNKERSETT, Esquire,
President of the Framji Cowasji
Committee, &c. &c. &c.

My DEAR SIR,

In thanking you for the favor of your note received last evening, I am sorry to inform you that the statement it affords of the Framji Cowasji Committee appears to me so little satisfactory that I should think it my duty to bring the matter before the next meeting of the Students' Literary and Scientific Society, and to consult with them what steps ought to be adopted by the Society for obtaining the advantages to which they are entitled, and which have been so long withheld from them by your Committee.

Our meeting has been postponed till Monday next, November 11th.

Believe me, my dear Sir,
Yours sincerely,

BOMBAY, 5th November 1861.   A. GRANT.

To

SIR ALEXANDER GRANT, BART.

MY DEAR SIR,

In reply to your note of the 5th instant, I beg to inform you that it has been laid before the Committee of the Framji Cowasji Institute and they consider that it calls for no remark beyond this acknowledgment in the present state of affairs.

Believe me,
My dear Sir,
Yours very sincerely,

JUGGUNNATH SUNKERSETT.

BOMBAY, 7th November 1861.

To

NARAYEN DINANATHJI, Esquire,

Secretary to the Framji Cowasji

Institute Committee.

Sir,

I have the honor to inform you that your letter of the 18th September last was brought before the notice of the Managing Committee of the Students' Literary and Scientific Society on Friday the 22nd ultimo, which was the first occasion of their holding a meeting since the date of your letter.

I am instructed by the Managing Committee to inform you that they are glad to learn that tenders have been invited for the building of the Framji Cowasji Institute, and they trust no delay may be suffered to take place in the accomplishment of so desirable a work.

The Managing Committee have authorized their Curator of minerals, &c., Mr. Ardasir Framji, to make over the whole of the collection to the Framji Cowasji Committee with a view to their being ultimately placed in the Victoria Museum.

With regard to the philosophical apparatus mentioned in your letter, I am instructed to request that this may be reserved for the use of the Students' Society as originally intended. This apparatus will be from time to time urgently required by the Students' Society for the illustration of lectures.

With regard to the proposal of the Framji Cowasji Committee to pay towards the Victoria Museum a sum of three or four thousand Rupees, I am insturcted to request that the Framji Cowasji Committee will keep this proposal in abeyance until such time as the Framji Cowasji Institute is completed both externally and internally, as it appears probable that all the available funds may be required for the purpose.

I have the honor to be,

Sir,

Your most obedient servant,

J. P. HUGHLINGS,

Secretary to the Students'

BOMBAY, 11*th December* 1861.   L. & S. Society.

———

To

PROFESSOR J. P. HUGHLINGS,

Secretary to the Students' Literary

and Scientific Society.

SIR,

With reference to your letter to my address, dated the 11th ultimo, I have been instructed by the Managing Committee of the Framji Cowasji Institute to inform you, that it is their intention to commence with the institute building with as little delay as possible, and that they in compliance with your request resolved not to make over the philosophical apparatus to the Victoria Museum.

With regard to your last paragraph, your Society may be assured, that whatsoever we may decide on will be the result of mature deliberation.

I have the honor to be,

Sir,

Your most obedient servant,

NARAYEN DINANATHJI,

BOMBAY, 20*th January* 1862.   Secretary.

To

NARAYEN DINANATHJI, Esquire,

Secretary to Framji Cowasji

Institute Committee.

Sir,

I beg to resign my seat as a Member of the Committee of the Framji Cowasji Institute.

I am,

Your obedient Servant,

RUSTOMJI JAMSETJI JEJEEBHOY.

Bombay, 20th January 1862.

To

ARDASIR FRAMJI, Esquire.

Sir,

I have the honor to transmit to you for your information and guidance, the following resolutions passed at a meeting of the Framji Cowasji Institute Committee, held on the 21st ultimo.

"That in compliance with the request of the Students' Literary and Scientific Society contained in their Secretary's letter of the 11th December 1861, the philosophical apparatus of the Framji Cowasji Institute be not made over to the Victoria Museum."

I have the honor to be,

Sir,

Your most obedient Servant,

NARAYEN DINANATHJI,

Bombay, 5th February 1862.   Secretary.

To

The MUNICIPAL COMMISSIONERS.

Gentlemen,

I have been informed that you are closing up the Bullock shed at the Framji Cowasji Tank, in order to prevent persons of low character making use of the shed as they do at present. You will oblige by informing me, whether you have any objection to allow materials intended for the Framji Cowasji Institute to be stored in the shed, after the walls have been built up. In this case, I would request that the side which opens in the premises of the Institute may be kept as it is. I engage to remove the materials within 24 hours' notice, and if necessary will be happy to pay a nominal rent for the use of the shed, but as the Institution is to be a public building I hope that for the short time the shed will be required for the use of the Institution, you will kindly permit the use of it free of charge.

I have the honor to be,

Sir,

Your most obedient Servant,

NARAYEN DINANATHJI,

Secretary to the
Framji Cowasji Institute.

Bombay, 16th July 1862.

CHAPTER XVII.

The laying of the Foundation Stone of the Framji Cawasji Institute.

The ceremony of laying the foundation stone of the Framji Cowasji Institute took place on Saturday the 22nd day of February 1862, afternoon, at five o'clock on the verge of the Framji Cowasji Tank, Esplanade, the Honorable Juggonnath Sunkersett, President of the Committee of the Institute, performing the ceremony. The President was assisted in the interesting ceremony by the members of the Committee as well as a large number of the friends and admirers of the late Framji Cowasji. Amongst those who were present, we noticed the Honorable W. E. Frere, the Honorable Rustomji Jamsetji Jejeebhoy, the Honorable the Nawab of Savanoor, the Honorable Mr. Tristram, Sir Alexander Grant, Bart., the Rev. Dr. Wilson, Dr. Birdwood, Messrs. Bomanji Hormusji, W. Crawford, T. C. Hope, R. S. Sinclair, G. Foggo, G. W. Terry, Munguldass Nuthoobhoy, Cursetji Nusserwanji Cama, Bomanji Framji Cama, Framji Nusserwanji, Sorabji Pestonji Framji, Nowroji Nanabhoy Framji, Dossabhoy Framji Cama, Narayen Dinnanathji, Venayekrow Juggonnathji, Jehangeer Nowroji, Cursetji Furdoonji, Vishwanath Narayen, Dossabhoy Framji Kurraka, Cowasji Edulji, Ardasir Framji, Pestonji Ruttonji Cola, Cursetji Rustomji Cama, &c., &c., &c. The place was decorated with flowers and leaves. The

Honorable Juggonnath Sunkersett commenced the proceedings with the following address :—

Gentlemen,

We are met here this afternoon to lay the foundation stone of a building, which on the death of the late Framji Cowasji, we resolved to dedicate to his memory under the name of the Framji Cowasji Institute. The duty has devolved on myself, as President of the Framji Cowasji Committee. For the credit of the occasion, I wish it had been entrusted to any one else; but so far as my personal feelings go, its discharge is a matter of great satisfaction to me, for the late Framji Cowasji was one of my best friends, and I am one of his oldest surviving friends, and his old Colleague in the late Board of Education, and other managing bodies. Indeed this day's duty has fallen to me, not simply because I am President of the Committee, but by reason also of the express wishes of the family of my lamented Friend. The building will contain a lecture room, a reading room and a laboratory. It was intended that a Museum of Natural History and Economic Products should be accommodated under the same roof; but the Victoria Museum being about to be erected, that idea has been abandoned; and the Committee's collection of minerals, rocks and fossils has been made over to the Government Central Museum. When the Victoria Museum shall be built, these with other Natural History specimens will be placed on one floor, while another will be devoted exclusively to economic articles, the former (it will be the gallery) to be denominated the Framji Cowasji Museum of Natural History. The Institution, as you are aware, is to be in connection with the Students' Literary and Scientific Society, and of the benefits it is likely to afford to that Society and the public at large, none can doubt. The style of the building is very plain, but suitable for the purpose for which it is designed. It is true that considerable delay has taken place in laying the foundation, and the Committee has suffered no little blame for this—and I must add undeservedly; for we have spared no exertions in giving effect to the wishes of the originators of the Institution. But all know the competition which exists in Bombay for good building sites, all know the numberless obstacles (each petty enough in itself) which must be overcome before a building can be commenced even after a site has been secured. We are satisfied then with our own conduct, and at the same time well aware that the criticism we have experienced has been prompted by the best of motives; we would here take the opportunity of thanking those from whom it came and all others who have sincerely desired to assist in bringing this undertaking to its present stage. The Speaker here stopped and laid the foundation stone when he resumed his address as follows :—

"MAY GOD BLESS THIS UNDERTAKING."

And now in conclusion let me say a word to my young friends, for whose special advantage this Institution is designed. Framji Cowasji was one of those whom you would call "old Bombay," and for my old friend and for that class of "old Bombay," I would express the hope that, when in the enjoyment of the benefits thus secured to you by them in this instance as well as in numerous others you may have a kindly thought for those to whom you are indebted for them.

Pan-sooparee and nosegays were then distributed, and the interesting ceremony was brought to a close by the Union Band, which was in attendance, striking up " God Save the Queen. "

The following is the Inscription on the Copperplate laid under the Foundation Stone :—

IN THE REIGN OF HER MOST GRACIOUS MAJESTY, VICTORIA.

AND UNDER THE VICEROYALTY OF

THE RIGHT HON'BLE C. JOHN, EARL CANNING,

GOVERNOR GENERAL OF INDIA,

HIS EXCELLENCY THE HON'BLE SIR G. RUSSEL CLERK,

BEING GOVERNOR OF BOMBAY ;

THE FOUNDATION STONE OF

THE FRAMJI COWASJI INSTITUTE

WAS LAID IN THE PRESENCE OF

THE FRIENDS AND ADMIRERS OF THE LATE

FRAMJI COWASJI, ESQUIRE,

BY THE HON'BLE JUGGONNATH SUNKERSETT,

ASSISTED

By the Members of the Committee of the said Institute, on Saturday the 22nd day of February, in the year of the Christian Era 1862 ; of Yeszdezard 1231 ; of Shalivan 1783; of Vicramaditya 1918 ; Hizri 1278 ; and of the Jewish year 5622.

May the Blessings of God Almighty Be Upon

THIS WORK.

www.ingramcontent.com/pod-product-compliance
Lightning Source LLC
Chambersburg PA
CBHW020534270326
41927CB00006B/570